# 400 YEARS OF TREMAYNES AT HELIGAN

by

IVOR J. HERRING

© Copyright Ivor J. Herring and the Publisher

ISBN 0 902660 268

All Rights Reserved. This book is protected by copyright.
No part of it may be reproduced, stored in a retreival system or transmitted
in any form or by any means electronic mechanical photocopying recording
or otherwise without the written permission of the author or publisher.

*First Published in 1999 by*
THE FEDERATION OF OLD CORNWALL SOCIETIES

*designed & printed by*

PARKER
⊡ *Creative digital design*

# ILLUSTRATION ACKNOWLEDGMENTS

The Author and Publisher would like to express their appreciation and grateful thanks to the following for allowing photographs and illustrations from their collections to be used in this book;

Cornwall Record Office for permission to use two of the Tremayne Documents, T1284/20/6 and X148.2. Copyright and Publication rights reserved.

To Terry Knight of the Local Studies Library at Redruth for permission to use two photographs E9267 and E9272 from The George Ellis Collection.

All the other photographs are from the collection of Robert E. Evans of Pentewan.

The map and other drawings were produced by the author.

# ABOUT THE AUTHOR

## Ivor J. Herring M.A.

Ivor Herring has a Cambridge History Degree for which he specialised in Political Science and Constitutional Law. After 10 years as a Master in two "Public Schools" he was for 28 years a Grammar School Headmaster.

Product of his Belfast years his book 'History of Ireland' was published by Murray (London) in 1937. Also in the late thirties, he did eight talks on Rural History for the B.B.C.

After 15 years lecturing to adult groups for London University, he was accorded the status of Senior Lecturer in Archaeology.

In his 70th year he came to live at Heligan, in 1978, and researched the Tremayne and Heligan manuscripts in the Cornwall County Record Office. Since his work on the manuscripts he has given talks to many various organisations on the History of Heligan, and he has also had several articles published in journals and magazines.

He has been a member of Pentewan Old Cornwall Society since 1978 and is now a Vice President, and in 1995 he was made a Cornish Bard taking the name Arethyor Heligan

## "Speaker of Heligan"

# ACKNOWLEDGMENTS


The bulk of my indebtness is to the Cornwall County Record Office where I spent long hours from 1978 onwards researching the manuscripts in the Tremayne collection. Especially the following;

| | | | |
|---|---|---|---|
| DDT | 823/2 | DDT | 2175 |
| | 828/7 | DDT | 2884-5 |
| DDT | 1284/20/ 3-6. | DDT | 2887-9 |
| DDT | 1284/120/18 | DDT | 2891 |
| DDT | 1573-4 | DDT | 2893-9 |
| DDT | 1764 | DDT | 2901 |
| DDT | 2153/1 | | |

Grateful thanks in appreciation for all my time spent there to the County Archivist, Christine North and all her staff at the Record Office. To the Federation of Old Cornwall Societies I also record my grateful thanks for publishing my manuscript on the Tremaynes of Heligan, and to the Federation's Publications Officer, Robert Evans for his help and encouragement.

Ivor Herring,
Heligan House,
St. Ewe,
Cornwall.

# Contents          Page

HELIGAN
13/4

# TREMAYNE ORIGINS

Available to us are two Tremayne pedigrees, one by J. Polsue in his 'Parochial History of Cornwall' Vol. I (1867), the other by Lt. Col. Vivian in 'The Visitations of the County of Cornwall' (1887). Polsue's starts with Perys Tremayne of Tremayne in St. Martin-in-Meneage, of the time of Edward I. Vivian goes back two generations earlier and he differs from Polsue as he lists Perys correctly as 'Perys de Tremayne', and the use of 'de Tremayne' continues down to Perys's grandson John de Tremayne M.P. in Edward III's reign. But the latter's younger brother is listed as Thomas Tremayne, of Carwithenack in Constantine. Thereafter the 'de' is dropped.

This seeming confusion is explained by the fact that the use of surnames developed slowly after the Norman Conquest, doubtless assisted by pressure from lawyers who needed accurate identification of folk, especially in days when so many were given Christian names of Biblical origin, Matthew, Mark, Luke, and John, especially John. Over the centuries surnames were invented, a variety of ploys being used. A John's son became Johnson and future generations were pegged to it. Other families produced an occupation surname, eg. Smith, and the smith's descendants were surnamed Smith even though they might not be employed in that craft. A man on the move could be given the surname of his village or town of origin. In the parish a man living on the fringe of a belt of trees could be surnamed Wood. Others could be surnamed after their residence. So we come to Tremayne. Tre (homestead, farm) is such a common prefix in Cornish names. So I interpret Tremayne as 'stone homestead' though Gill and Colwill in their 1986 book The Saints Way in a list of common elements in Cornish Place Names give as an example for 'Men, Mayn' (stone) Tremaine with their meaning 'Farm at the Stone'.

Whatever the translation we have the family Tremayne deriving its surname from its home of long ago, and after the reign of Edward III the records no longer have 'de' or 'of' Tremayne, but simply Tremayne.

Tremayne as a farmstead home still exists in St. Martin -in-Meneage, a quarter of a mile south of the Helford River, and so just in the Lizard Peninsula. One and a half miles and two miles west of the villages of Helford and Manaccan. It is of course the modern 'descendant' of the medieval Tremayne. I was invited there by the present owner Norman Bennett through the kind offices of his neighbour, my friend Sq. Ldr. George Witherwick, the skilled developer of the Trelean landscape. My visit was a special joy to me as Norman Bennett chose my eighty fifth birthday, 13th July 1993, in which to make my territorial contact with the Tremaynes of the Middle Ages, the family I had been studying since my arrival in Cornwall as a Heligan resident, in 1978, after which I enjoyed long hours in the Cornwall Records Office with the large collection of Tremayne manuscripts.

To return to the Tremayne pedigree, the grandson of Perys was Thomas Tremayne, doubtless a younger son as he was listed not as resident at Tremayne but at Carwithenack in Constantine, on the north side of the Helford River. He married Isabella, daughter and heiress of Trenchard of Collacombe, Lamerton (Devon). Widowed Isabella remarried to Sir John Damerell. According to Polsue, Sir John entailed several estates on her Tremayne children. So there emerged a Tremayne family in West Devon. That offshoot of the Cornish Tremaynes developed its own status in Devon independent of the parent family in St. Martin-in-Meneage, Cornwall. Isabella's Tremayne son Nicholas married Joan, heiress of Sir John Dodscombe, and Nicholas's son Thomas (M.P. for Tavistock and South Molton 1489) married Elizabeth Carew - on that

# TREMAYNE HOUSES — 14th to 19th C

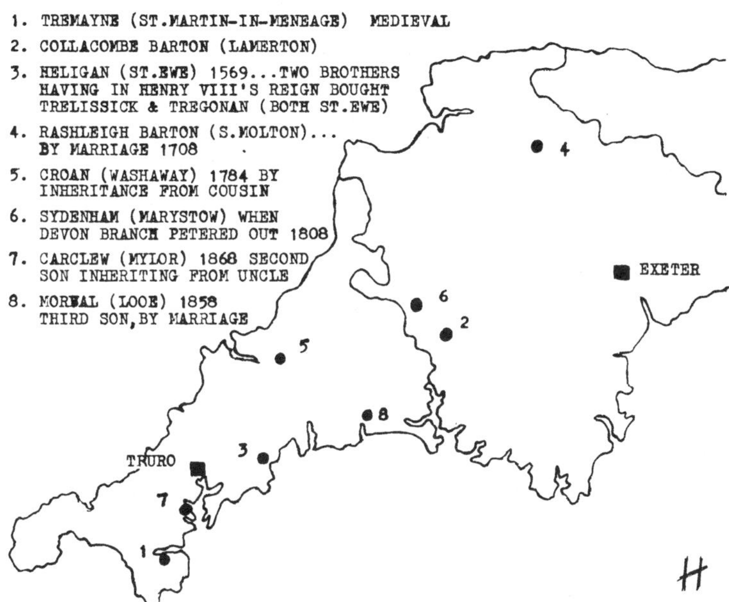



Polsue and Vivian differ, Polsue describing Elizabeth as a daughter of Peter, Baron Carew, while Vivian makes her daughter of Thomas Carew. Thus the Devonian Tremayne marriages stabilised them at Collacombe, just a little over two miles from the Tamar county boundary, as part of the local landed gentry. But one gets the impression that, having been Devonianised, the Tremaynes in Devon leaned towards Cornwall, for we find Joan, daughter of the above mentioned M. P. Thomas Tremayne, married Sir Richard Edgecumbe and today's National Trust devotees will recall at Cotehele the heraldic panels in the hall include the device of the Tremaynes. Cotehele, though in Cornwall, is a good fifty miles north east of the parental family home in the parish of St. Martin-in-Meneage, in Cornwall.

The Tremayne Devon home, Collacombe, one and a half miles west south west of the village of Lamerton - its church has a fine Tremayne monument - was and is fine enough. Arthur Mee's Devon describes it as 'a fine Elizabethan farmhouse ...with a beautiful plaster ceiling and a huge window containing three hundred and sixty five oblong and diamond shaped panes, one for every day of the year'. But to this more was added in the 17th century. Sydenham by Edmund Tremayne (he died in 1690) when he wed Arabella, daughter and sole heiress of Sir Edward Wise of Sydenham in Marystow. Again to quote Arthur Mee on the village of Sydenham Damerel ...'outside the village is Sydenham House, a typical Elizabethan mansion with a fine carved staircase, only one and a half miles south west of Collacombe Barton.'

It was from the Devonian branch of the Tremaynes and not from the Cornish that Tremaynes came to the parish of St. Ewe in Cornwall. An early Tudor Devonian Tremayne was Richard, (married to Jane, daughter of Oliver Wise), described in the pedigrees as of Upcott and of Tregoddick in South Petherwin. South Petherwin just south west of Launceston suggests to me again, (probably without reason) that the Devonian Tremaynes leaned towards a return to Cornwall. This Richard had five sons of whom the third son John, and the fifth son Sampson, migrated to St. Ewe parish. John bought Tregonan, not far from the parish boundary and near Trevithick Barton, approximately a mile from St. Ewe Churchtown. John was to die without heir in 1570 and he left Tregonan to his nephew Richard, son of his elder brother. Sampson seemingly first bought Trelissick between Trevithick and Tubbs Mill: he went further for in 1536 he acquired half the manor of Heligan from the Hals family of Efford. Thirty one years later, in 1567,

# SUGGESTED EVOLUTION of HELIGAN

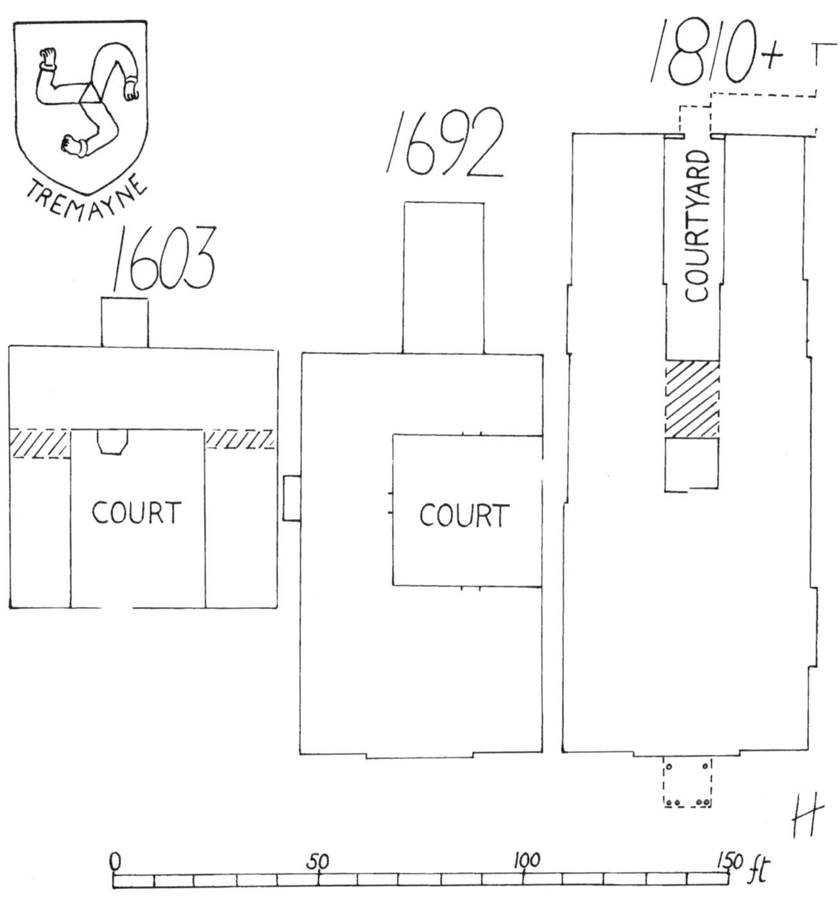

he bought from Richard Grenville of Penheale, 'a tenement in Hillygan, Hyllygon Mill etc.' (a quote from Polsue's pedigree of the Tremaynes). Thus Sampson became the owner of the whole of the Heligan Manor. Dying in 1593, he had not built at Heligan, so presumably he lived in the farmhouse of Heligan Barton. Tremayne building at Heligan was to come with his son, William. So Heligan, becoming Tremayne property in the reign of Queen Elizabeth I, remained so into the reign of Queen Elizabeth II.

# HELIGAN I ~ 1603

Sampson Tremayne retained his Devonian family background by his marriage to Margaret, daughter and heiress of Downing (Tredowne, Devon).

His son, William, Heligan's owner, reinforced his acquired Cornishness by marrying, at Truro in August 1579, Ann, daughter and heiress of John Pye of Lanzearth, St. Stephen-in-Brannel, a place destined in the future to be part of the China Clay 'lunar landscape'. One wonders why they did not marry in the church of St. Stephen-in-Brannel with its splendid Norman font in the distinctive Bodmin style, with uprights topped by crowned heads and supporting a bowl, the decoration on which was fancifully described by Betjeman as of 'Tiger Tim and other wild beasts'.

The major undertaking by William, who died in 1614, was to build the first Tremayne Heligan. Call it 'Heligan I 1603'. Its plan is in the collection of the Tremayne manuscripts held by the Cornwall Record Office, (DDT 1284/20/3).

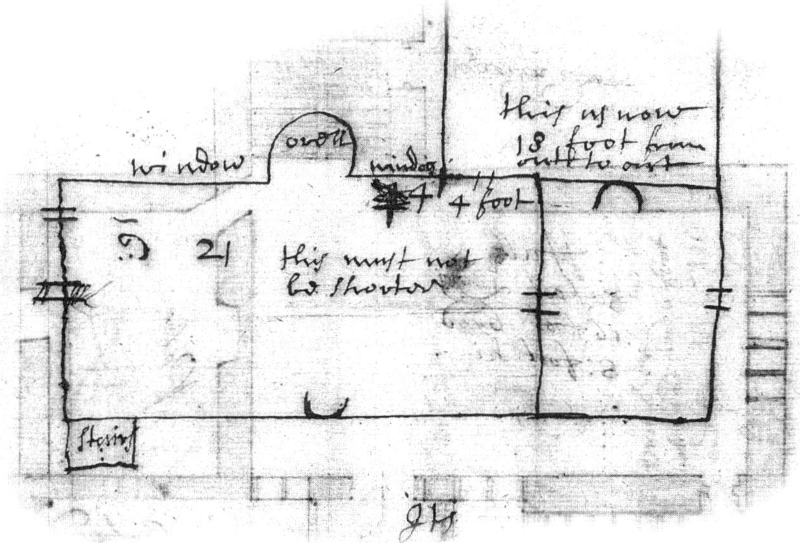



*Plan of house 1735. (Cornwall Record Office DDT 1284/20/6)*

The design is based on a square, each side 63ft, with buildings on three sides of a courtyard 41ft x 29ft. Initially I took the 'Garden Door' of that courtyard to be the main approach as it was opposite the Hall Door. Possibly I was too speculative, overinfluenced by the fact that the Record Office treated the document as vertically disposed. Later, after further study of the designers notes, I realised the main entrance was up seven steps between the Hall and the 'Siler' (Cellar) to reach the Hall Door. The plan was originally horizontally disposed. That would make the Court Yard facing south east looking down to Mevagissey.

Of an antiquarian interest is the late Elizabethan spelling on the house plan:- Paler (Parlour), Kichen, Siler (Cellar), Lador (Larder), bred (broad), hi (high).

William Tremayne's Heligan comes into the period dubbed by W .G. Hoskins (1953) as the GREAT REBUILD, late Elizabethan and early Jacobean, when the medieval building concepts in vogue came under scrutiny, sometimes taking note of continental developments. I am referring to the dwellings of the gentry and the middle classes. The result of the re-think was often greater convenience and comfort.

Already in the late Middle Ages a Hall House indicated upper middle class or gentry ownership. But William's Heligan, built around its Hall (30ft x 16ft) was for its time modern in the sense that it did not extend upwards to the roof. It was listed as 8ft high, and above it was a second floor containing a Dining Room, (21ft x 16ft) and a Bedroom. Though the designer favoured us with no elevation drawing of the house, so that its appearance is difficult to deduce, he did add in the margin a basic elevation sketch across the 16ft (the narrower width) of the Dining Room above the Hall.

Reverting to details of the Hall (windows for the Hall flanked the Hall Door) looking out into the Courtyard, and

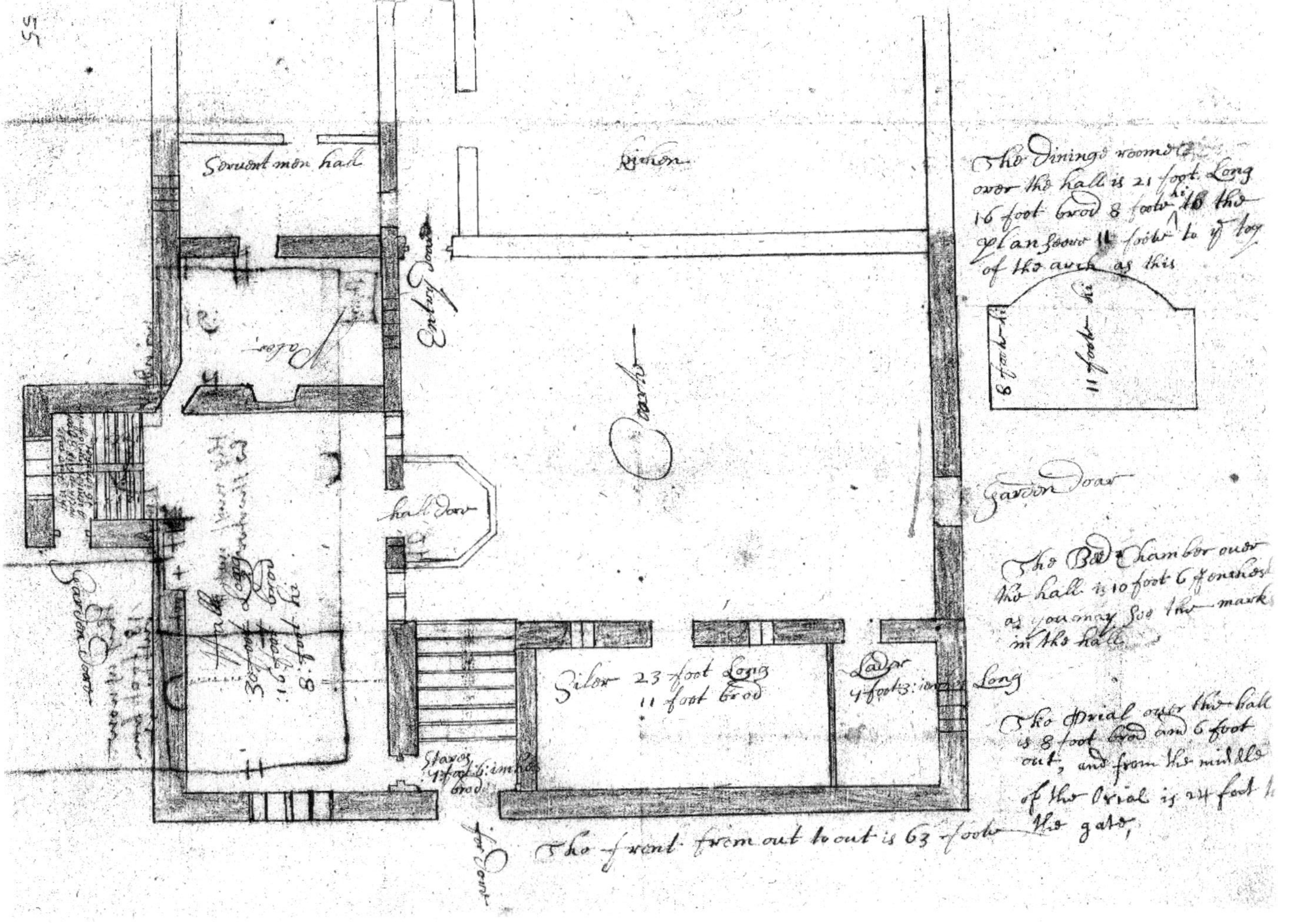

55
6
Servuont men hall
Kichon
Entry Doar
Poler
hall Door
Coorht
Silor 23 foot Long 11 foot brod
Lader 4 foot 3: inch Long
Staires 4 foot 6: inch brod
Garden Doar
for Door
Hall 30 foot Long 16 foot brod 8 foot hi
The dininge roome over the hall is 21 foot Long 16 foot brod 8 foot hi the plansoor 11 foot to y top of the arch as this
8 foot hi
11 foot hi
Garden Doar
The Bed Chambor over the hall is 10 foot 6 fonchos as you may see the mark in the hall
The Orial over the hall is 8 foot brod and 6 foot out, and from the middle of the Orial is 24 foot to the gate,
The front from out to out is 63 foote

windows were also in the outside wall. The Hall fireplace is shown in the back wall nearly opposite the Hall Door.

In front of the Hall Door on the Courtyard side is shown in the drawing a five sided arrangement which could be interpreted as an entrance platform. A marginal note indicated it was topped by an Oriel (a word absorbed into English from Old French and meaning Porch). That Oriel could have been supported by brackets or corbels jutting out from the Hall wall. A note in the plan's margin gives the Oriel the same size as what I called the 'entrance platform',(8ft x 6ft) and it also specifies its mid-point was 24ft to the gate (that is the main gate through the front wall just before the stairs).

There remain other puzzles about the Hall.

(a) There is the question of levels. To the left, as one comes into the site's Front entrance facing the Stairs, there is shown a door into the Hall. How does one interpret and harmonise the levels? Do those stairs go up or down?

(b) On the plan in the corner of the Hall, adjacent to the fireplace is shown a double set of stairs, with an exit labelled as another Garden Door. Can one interpret this part of the drawing as one stairway out from the Hall to the Garden, and the other up to a second storey? To turn to more certainty:- the Hall in the plan is flanked by a Parlour (10ft x 16ft) entered from a corner of the Hall. It has a fireplace and a window looking out into the Courtyard. Through the wall opposite the Parlour's fireplace is a doorway into the Servantmen's Hall, (7ft x 16ft), also backed by a larger room, the purpose of which is not specified. The Servantmen's Hall was seemingly unheated, and was lit by one window opposite which was an exit door giving access across the back Entry to a very large Kitchen, (35ft by probable 18ft). Indeed to me the surprising feature of Heligan I is that the Kitchen together with the Cellar (23ft x 11ft) and its adjacent Larder (7ft x 11ft), both on the opposite side of the Courtyard to the Kitchen, are area-wise more extensive than the Tremaynes' Hall and Parlour.

We get from the plan no evidence of any bedroom other than the one beside the Dining Room over the Hall. Doubtless there were other bedrooms not shown on the plan. Confusion is added to one's musings when the pedigree by Vivian gave William a goodly batch of children (Polsue agreed.) Heligan I, to take account of the family and resident servants, needed plenty of bedrooms. One must assume though the plan gives no indication of a storey over more than the Hall, that there were bedrooms over the Parlour and the various domestic rooms.

Ten years after building Heligan I, William Tremayne drew up his Will, February 15th, 1613, just a year before his death. Much of his cramped writing I cannot read, and there is also the problem of 1613 spelling. The Will differs from the printed pedigrees as it names fewer children, (one can proffer sundry reasons for that). The sons named in order were Oliver, Thomas and John. William frequently stated Oliver was his executor and once referred to him as his heir. Perhaps Oliver and Thomas must have pre-deceased their father or debarred for some reason, as we find the third son John, succeeded at Heligan. But here the published pedigrees create confusion by seeming vagueness. The new owner of Heligan, John's birth is listed by Vivian as 1619, four years after his father's death! One explanation could be that the inheriting John was not a son, but a grandson. But both published pedigrees agree in stating that it was this John who added to Heligan: Polsue even dates the work 1637, though so far I have found no documentary proof. Perhaps he added bedrooms.

Reverting to that 1613 Will of William Tremayne, in it he names John, and John's first wife, Jane née Dart of Pentewan. And William, after specifying money given to the poor of St. Ewe and Broadwoodwidger in Devon, he bequethed to his wife Ann, 'two feather beds and their furniture, two pans and a cauldron, two pots, a half dozen pewter dishes, a table bord and a form'. Seemingly there was in the early 17th century a dictatorial treatment of daughters by the family, for example, in his Will, William gave Margaret and Priscilla £50 each, each to be paid on marriage, "if she marries by consent of her mother and brothers or any two of them". The youngest daughter Judith was not so mentioned, but was to receive 'her bed and furniture that she lies on', a yearly allocation of forty shillings and William's desire, 'my loving wife during her life to give maintenance to the said Judith'. Perhaps Judith was frail: indeed she died soon after her father, in 1619. Apart from donations of money and property to his sons, William gave John his black mare and Thomas his little nag.

# CIVIL WAR TIME'S

John, the inheritor of Heligan, appears in St. Ewe Church documents; in 1624 he was with his fellow churchwarden making an inventory of church property; in 1659 he was 'Overseer of the Poor'.

So John Tremayne lived through the division of Britain caused by the developing clash between the monarchy and parliament-led opposition, (when Cornwall generally supported the King), through the Commonwealth when Cromwell was dominant, and he saw the Restoration of the monarchy in 1660. He also experienced the local anxiety over danger from the sea. James I had allowed English naval strength to decline, and Dunkirk had become a base for Channel raiders. One Dunkirk raider seized four ships off the Lizard in one haul, two of them local, from Looe and Fowey. Algerian and Moroccon pirates were also active; in ten days of the year 1625 they seized twenty seven ships.

But of course the main preoccupation of the Tremaynes was the Civil War 1642-1649. Inevitably the family's participation was not by John, in his late fifties when the war began, but by his son Lewis, born c1620. Though the normal assessment is that Cornwall supported Charles I in the Civil War, not all the leading Cornish families were Royalists. Lord Robartes of Lanhydrock was a keen Parliamentarian, as were Alexander Carew, Sir Richard Buller and John St. Aubyn. Heligan's Tremaynes were Royalist.

When Hopton and Sir Bevil Grenville managed to transform the Cornish Royalist troops from untrained bands into a formidable fighting force, I get the impression that it was almost on the same basis as in the Jacobite Rebellion a century later when the clansmen followed their chiefs; Cornish landowners could lead their tenants and servants. There is a list of Lewis Tremayne's 1646 "regiment" of foot; He had been elevated to the rank of Colonel; a list doubtless containing local names, but nothing has been discovered of his involvement till the Royalist cause was on the wane.

One has to assume that he and other local men fought on Braddock Down, January 19th, 1643, five months after the start of the war, when the Cornish Royalists broke the Parliamentary army which had advanced from the Tamar crossing, and had reached west of Liskeard. The Royalist losses were light but when a collection for the wounded was made at St. Ewe Church, the Tremayne accounts show that squire John Tremayne, Lewis's father, contributed two shillings and six pence. Resisting the temptation to consider this amount derisory, we must remember centuries of inflation and the possibility that Lewis paid his own men, at that stage at least. It was in 1643 that the King's letter of thanks to the Cornish was copied and enlarged to hang on church walls; St. Ewe Church had one but it has disappeared.

In July 1644, after the Cornishmen had fought outside the county and as far as Bath and Bristol, the see-sawing campaigns saw the Parliamentary Earl of Essex reaching mid-Cornwall, only to find himself hemmed in between Lostwithiel and Fowey by four Royalist forces, with the King himself at Boconnoc. Could it have been in this phase that Colonel Lewis Tremayne's house at Kestle was raided by a Parliamentary squad?

The Tremayne manuscripts remain largely silent about Colonel Lewis till the stage of Royalist decline, the men tending to lose discipline when faced by the New Model Army of Fairfax. We do find occasional references e.g. Sir Richard Grenville writing from Torrington on December 1st, 1645, to his "dear cousin" Lewis, giving him the task of defending a Tamar crossing; "In pursuance of his highness directions I have appoynted that drawbridges be made upon the several bridges uppon the river Tamar to secure the County of Cornwall as well as from the Rebells as such unruly troopers as doe plunder and abuse the county. These are therefore to will and authorise you with your own regiment of olde soldiers to keepe and mayntayne troop guards on Bridge-rule and North Tamerton Bridges and to keep your small guards as you shall find cause on all fordable places as you are to fortifie on the Cornish side by digging deep trenches to receive water and by making of breastworks that may prevent any horse or footmen to passe through the river. And on the said two bridges (viz Bridge-rule and North Tamerton bridges) you are to cause two good and sufficient drawe bridges to be made and built to be secured and taken upp by the guards on the Cornish side..."

Colonel Lewis was also authorised to impress local workmen for the jobs. Soon another letter cut down the geographical extent of the work, and authorised Lewis to extract from the Hundreds of Black Torrington and Stratton money for the payment and maintenance of workmen conscripted.

On December 4th, 1645, Grenville reported to Lewis an enemy advance to Crediton with two thousand horse and foot. Lewis was to draw together his trained soldiers at Stratton; the object was to get them into "a fitt position for a speedy march". The march was to be a retreat.

Way back, in the spring of 1645, the King had made Prince Charles commander of the Royal forces in the West Country. It was a propaganda move rather than a military one for the Prince was only fifteen years of age; he had been allotted an advisory Council on which Sir Edward Hyde and Lord Hopton were prominent. As the Parliamentary forces advanced through Devon, the Prince and his Council withdrew westward to Launceston and soon to Pendennis Castle. In March 1646, with Parliament's commander, Fairfax, pressing westward, and when on 16th April, 1646, Royalist St. Michael's Mount surrendered, the Prince removed to Scilly, later to Jersey and still later to France.

One wonders what Colonel Lewis thought of his military superior, Sir Richard Grenville. A modern historian, F. E. Halliday in his book 'A History of Cornwall' (1959), castigates him as 'the savage and rapacious bully' though he recalls Grenville's military experience in Germany and Ireland. Even worse Grenville could not work with a fellow commander, Lord Goring, (Halliday's assessment of Goring is "dissolute and unpredictable"), and when, in January 1646, Lord Hopton was made Royalist supreme commander, Grenville would not obey him. So he was arrested and incarcerated at St. Michael's Mount, an appropriate punishment but unpopular with the Cornish troops, for Grenville, unlike the other commanders, was Cornish and a brother of the esteemed Sir Bevil Grenville, commander of the foot in the past days when Royalist forces were in the ascendant.

For Colonel Lewis Tremayne the records come to his part in the last ditch defence of Pendennis Castle, March-August 1646. There exist for comparison three useful lists, two of them entirely of St. Ewe parish. The first is pre-Civil War, the Cornwall Protestation Return of 1641, at a time when King Charles I and Parliament were increasingly "at odds". Parliament was requiring the population to sign the Protestation, a composite declaration, of support for the Protestant faith, of opposition to the Pope, of support for the King, for the privileges of Parliament and for the legal rights of the King's subjects. It has been described as a roundabout way of defending Parliament's privileges without seeming to be anti-King.

The Return was for men only. One hundred and eighty

eight in St. Ewe parish signed their assent. The signatures of John Tremayne and his son Lewis were there, and that of Lewis's brother Philip. At the end of the document it was revealed that three St. Ewe men refused to sign, in addition to, William Fowler, Oliver Tremayne, and his son John. The published pedigrees do not always date Tremaynes, not in the main line of succession or give other useful details. So I leave this Oliver and John unidentified. Whoever they were, they were wary of that 1641 ploy by Parliament.

The second St. Ewe parish list is undated but titled, "A note of the soldiers in His Majesty's Service" …seemingly a list of local men joining the Royal forces in the Civil War. Were they the men available to Lewis Tremayne when he went to war? The main list is of thirty nine men but another ten are added, described as "Able men". Twenty four of the thirty nine appear on the 1641 Protestation Return; a few more have the same surnames as those listed then.

The third list I used is really two lists. "A perfect list of Colonel Tremayne his soldiers in Pendennis Castle", May 1646, with fifty nine names, and, "A list of Colonel Tremaynes officers and soldiers", thirty two names, including that of Colonel Lewis…on the first page. In the bottom right hand corner of that first page is a list of payments.

| | |
|---|---|
| *1 Col* | *7. 17. 6* |
| *1 Col* | *7. 17. 6* |
| *1 Capt* | *2. 12. 6* |
| *3 Lefts* | *2. 2. 6* |
| *2 Ensigns* | *1. 1. 0* |
| *1 Q m* | *14. 0* |
| *Sould 43* | *4. 6. 0* |
| | *26. 10. 6* |

Wages? And for what period of time?

The second page lists twenty six more names; six are listed as sick, five as dead, and two as "run".

What seems to be apparent is that Colonel Lewis in Pendennis commanded not just his local men but a composite lot, some of whom had places of origin listed …only one named as from St. Ewe.

The background to this is Lord Hopton's decision that the situation of his Royalist force had become hopeless when Fairfax's Parliamentary army reached Tregony. On 9th March, 1646, Hopton asked Fairfax for a meeting at Tresillian Bridge to discuss terms for surrender. Yet he planned, while surrendering, to save St. Michael's Mount and Pendennis Castle. He sent two hundred men to the Mount and eight hundred and sixty to Pendennis under the command of John Arundell of Trerice, "John for the King". Hopton hoped to get stores and provisions from Truro down to Pendennis if Arundell could find boats. Hopton's force surrendered to Fairfax on 12th March, so the Parliament forces were able to impose a tight grip on Pendennis as they were now in control of St. Mawes and of the near part of Falmouth, Arwenack just west of Pendennis. Fairfax, busy elsewhere, left the siege to Colonel Hammond. Arundell had already rejected a call to surrender Pendennis on the 18th March, but he and his Council, of which Colonel Lewis Tremayne was a member, were fully aware of the perilous nature of their situation, unable to get supplies except by sea from France and Ireland, and constantly under fire from Hammond's batteries. Yet on the Parliamentary side there was no under-rating of the Royalists; their leaders seemed "the most desperate persons, and the violentest enemies that the Parliament hath in this Kingdom".

Back in Heligan John Tremayne, father of Colonel Lewis, encountered stress over and above his anxiety for his son and the Royalist cause. On 24th May, 1646, John complained that he had been arrested on a warrant of Colonel Fortescue and imprisoned at Penryn because Colonel Lewis in a sorty out of Pendennis had taken two prisoners, civilians, "for that they stood affected to the Parliament". Fortescue categorised Lewis's action "to be very uncivil" in contrast with his own treatment of pro-Royalists. He complained of Lewis's refusal to deliver them up and that he dealt "rigidly with them".

A responding letter from Lewis to Colonel Fortescue stated that he knew of no law allowing the imprisonment of a father for what his son was alleged to have committed. He added; "I neither took the prisoners mentioned nor uncivilly treated them". Earlier Arundell on April 17th, rejected Hammond's call to surrender, citing honour and loyalty to the King. Again on April 30th, he rejected a surrender call from Vice-Admiral Batten blockading by sea.

On June 7th, Batten captured a relief ship sent on the orders of the Prince of Wales, still then in Jersey; it carried supplies including barrels of beef, salted hogs, cider and gunpowder.

Two months later Arundell and his Council accepted that they could not continue the defence of Pendennis. There were deserters, the garrison suffered from hunger and plague, and only one small boat with provisions had slipped through the blockade. Though the Royalist guns continued to fire, Arundell accepted the inevitable. He treated with Vice-Admiral Batten and Colonel Fortescue on 15th August, and the next day signed surrender terms. So on the 17th August, the Royalist garrison marched out with full honours of war; "with their horses, compleat Arms and other Equipages, with flying colours, Trumpets sounding, Drums beating, Matches lighted at both ends, Bullets in their Mouths, and every Soldier Twelve charges of Powder with Bullets and Match proportionable". The

Royalist officers and men had numbered eight hundred and eighty six, but there were some left in Pendennis for it was said between three hundred and four hundred were too ill to march out, and that figure included two hundred women and children.

The terms were generous, the Royalist being granted £500 towards the care of their sick as well as supplies for their journey. Later the story was told that Colonel Lewis Tremayne from the Pendennis siege, "made almost a miraculous escape by swimming over from one of the block houses to Trefusis Point, through all the enemy's fire". He suffered much, and was forced to keep close during most of the usurpation. I noted that story surfaced in the opening decade of the 19th century, over a century and a half after the alleged event. I found it in R. Polwhele's 'History of Cornwall' (1803-8), and I have seen it nowhere else. I doubt the story for two reasons. Firstly, Colonel Lewis was one of the five officers adding signatures to that of Arundell on the surrender document. Secondly, there still exists in the County Record Office a pass signed by Colonel Fortescue and Admiral Batten:-

*"Suffer the bearer hereof Colonel Lewis Tremayne with his servants, armes, horses and goods quietly to passe unto St. Ewe or any other place within the pliants pts or beyond the seas about their pticuler ynploymes wthout any search plunder or Injury they also beinge to have the benefitt of the articles upon the Surrender of the Castell of Pendennis.*
*Given under our hands this 17th of August 1646.*

*Rich ffortescue*
*Will Batten*

*To all officers, souldiers, and others whom they concerne."*

I cannot conceive that an officer allegedly escaped from the siege would be in Pendennis in its final days and equipped with a pass from the victors commanders.

So Royalist Lewis Tremayne had to sit out painful years resulting from defeat not only in Cornwall but throughout the country. In 1649 he had to endure news of the execution of the King and the formation of the Commonwealth.

He had to keep his head down. But he was not on the list of Cornish Royalists paying fines to avoid having their estates sequestered; the explanation is simple - Heligan was still owned by his father, John Tremayne, who died in the year 1665.

There was Royalist plotting countered by Commonwealth agents gathering information which often led to preventive arrests. In 1655, Royalists agents planned a series of risings; only one took place involving the proclamation of King Charles II at Blandford, Dorset, and a raid at Salisbury. It had little support and ended in surrender. But it looks as if Cornish Royalists were "in the know", for shortly before the Salisbury raid well known Royalists including Lewis Tremayne met at Trerice, Arundell's home. They were also in touch with Prince Charles.

So seemingly the Tremaynes of Heligan avoided major trouble, but the church in St. Ewe had its shock for its rector John Smith was listed among the ejected Anglican clergy in Cornwall. John Smith in the Rectorial records is described as instituted in 1638 and succeeded on his death by George Brulon in 1670. Perhaps he was reinstalled with the restoration of the Monarchy.

So no major trouble for the Heligan Tremaynes but irritations. During the Commonwealth John and Lewis had to go to Truro to give details of their estate real and personal. And there survives a receipt for £5 paid by them "as moiety of a tax charged on them by the Court appointed by the Lord Protector (Cromwell) for securing the peace of the Commonwealth". Watch was being kept on Lewis's movements for in August 1659, John Tremayne reported to the St. Ewe constable that his son Lewis and wife were then lodging at Heligan, and he declared no knowledge of their future movements.

In 1660 the Monarchy returned in the person of King Charles II. In July 1660, the King ordered that Colonel Lewis Tremayne should be installed as Lieutenant-Governer of St. Mawes. Was the Certificate of Character, signed by nine notables including Arundell, connected with this appointment? To quote it;- Colonel Lewis Tremayne was "one of the first that tooke up armes in his late Majesties service and one of the last that layd them down…that he never had the reputation of a cruell ill natured insolent or Tyrannical person in Command or Conversation".

In November 1662, Lewis gave a letter of attorney to lawyer Hoblin empowering him to receive for him any money granted as compensation for his support of the Monarchy.

With father John's death in 1665, Lewis inherited Heligan, destined to be his for some twenty one years. Lewis had married Mary Carew, daughter and co-heiress of John Carew of Penwarne, Mevagissey. They had a sizeable family of which Charles born in 1650, was to become vicar of St. Austell. Charles's brother John, (birth date not recorded in the pedigrees printed) was destined to be knighted and King's Serjeant-at-Law.

Colonel Lewis's last years were seemingly not entirely satisfying for in May 1679, he asked his son John to find out if there was any chance that; "the King's old officers may be remembered and not like hounds past hunting turned of the kennel without provision for meate and lodging". Had the seeming financial compensation mentioned in 1662 not materialised or deemed inadequate?

Colonel Lewis died in 1685. The detailed Inventory of his Goods and Chattels made in 1685 is worth studying, but is too voluminous to republish here. It totalled £1662.4s.4d. a sizeable figure for those days. Of that £400 was for his wearing apparel, money, jewels, rings, watches. He had property in Cuby £250, and in St. Just-in-Roseland £55, a house in St. Mawes £30, two tenements at Gorran £20, a house at Probus £10. Also properties in the tin bounds of St. Margarets and Polgooth, together £50.

Manifestly the apparent shortage of bedrooms suggested by the scantily detailed plan of Heligan I 1603, had been corrected. Lewis had bedding in a chamber leading off from the Dining Room, doubtless the bedroom over the Hall in Heligan I. Bedding was in the chamber over the parlour; two beds in a chamber over the buttery, two more over the entry, beds in the kitchen chamber, in the garret, two beds in the servant maids chamber and three in two chambers over the cellar.

So the list rectifies the impression given by the plan of Heligan I.

The farm attached to the house was well stocked; crops of wheat, barley, oats, getting on for two hundred sheep and between forty and fifty cattle.

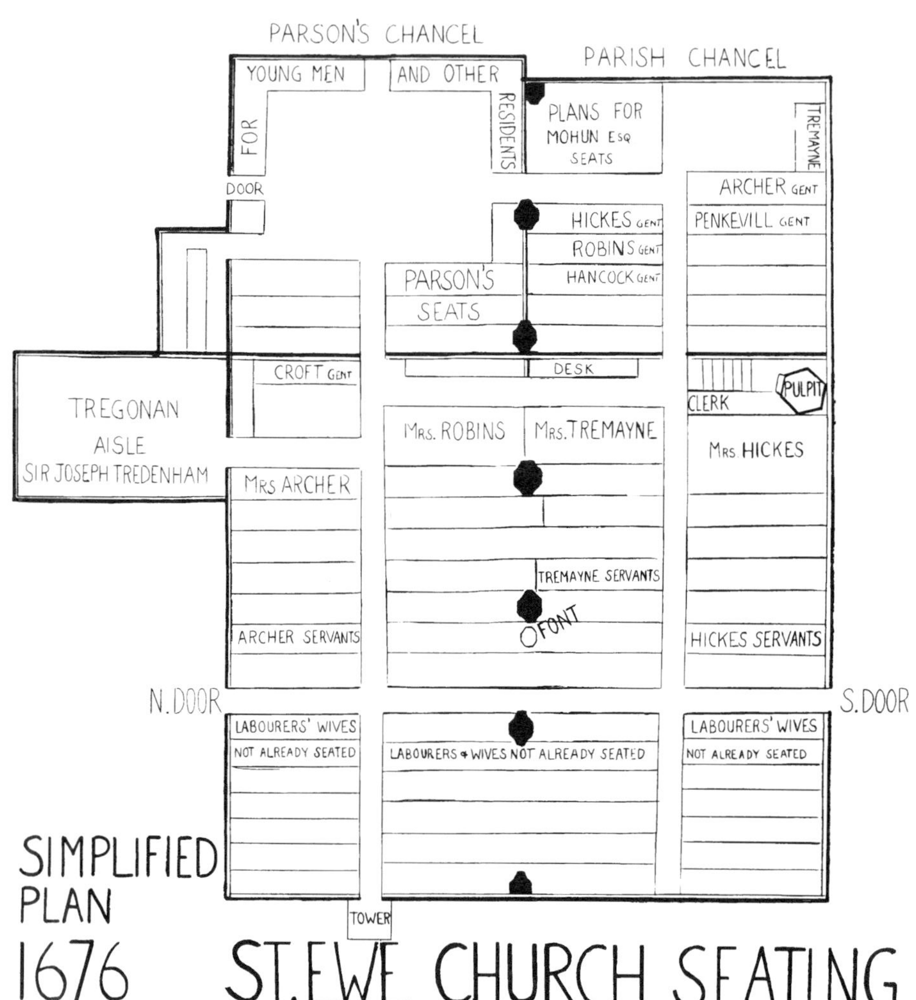

PARSON'S CHANCEL
PARISH CHANCEL
YOUNG MEN
AND OTHER
RESIDENTS
FOR
PLANS FOR
MOHUN ESQ
SEATS
TREMAYNE
DOOR
ARCHER GENT
PENKEVILL GENT
HICKES GENT
ROBINS GENT
HANCOCK GENT
PARSON'S
SEATS
CROFT GENT
DESK
CLERK
PULPIT
TREGONAN
AISLE
SIR JOSEPH TREDENHAM
MRS. ROBINS
MRS. TREMAYNE
MRS. HICKES
MRS ARCHER
TREMAYNE SERVANTS
FONT
ARCHER SERVANTS
HICKES SERVANTS
N. DOOR
S. DOOR
LABOURERS' WIVES
NOT ALREADY SEATED
LABOURERS & WIVES NOT ALREADY SEATED
LABOURERS' WIVES
NOT ALREADY SEATED
SIMPLIFIED
PLAN
1676
TOWER
ST. EWE CHURCH SEATING
NAMES RELEVANT TO ARTICLE ONLY GIVEN

# THE SECOND TREMAYNE HELIGAN 1692

It is perhaps a trifle bizarre to end the section of this account of Tremayne Heligan built around the Civil War and taking it on to the death of Colonel Lewis Tremayne in 1685… and then reversing the advancing chronicle by going back to 1676 and describing St. Ewe Church and its flock at that date. This account is reproduced here from the 'Old Cornwall Journal Vol. XI. No. 1 1991', with the approval of the editor.

The reason for this unorthodox behaviour can be explained by the realisation that in the 17th century a Cornish family was more than the residents of a house and the exploiters of their farm-land; they were a family intimately involved with their local church and not just for Sunday services. And for the departed Colonel Lewis there was his acute experience of the inter-relation of Church and State, for not only had his monarch been put to death, but also Archbishop Laud in 1645. And date wise the Church would not have changed in such a brief span. Nor the families mentioned.

## IN CHURCH 1676: A CORNISH EXAMPLE.

All Saints Church in the little village of St. Ewe near Mevagissey is much visited. Folk come to see its fine 15th or early 16th century screen, its 18th century monuments, and its three hatchments (two described by me in Old Cornwall Spring 1988 issue). Outside they look at a feature exotic for Cornwall, a broached spire, a stray from the East Midlands where that architectural device was invented and became fashionable in those parts. Perhaps too they look at the Atwell tombstone near the gate since we put on a special service on 4th May 1989, to revive the memory of the famous rector of St. Ewe who died on

4th May 1617, a man lovingly described in the '1602 Survey of Cornwall' by Richard Carew of Antony.

We have now added to the interest by hanging on the south wall near the font a framed transcript of the 1676 seating plan of the church, (in my copying I "translated" it into modern script to make it readable by visitors). The original is in the County Record Office, and the copy is on the wall with the approval of the County Archivist. The document, measuring 1ft 9in. by 1ft 5in., was drawn up following the instructions of the then Bishop of Exeter, and I have left two small portions unmodernised - the signatures of curate, churchwardens and four assenting parishoners, which I have traced. Traced also, top-left hand corner, the alternative spellings of the parish name "St. Ewe alias St. Tue, alias Eva. In the early 18th century the St. Ewe incumbent communicated with the bishop under the heading of "St. Tue". And still today local pronunciation could cause a visitor to write it down as St. Tue. I can produce another variant when once the Inland Revenue wrote to me at Stewe!

The response to the bishop's order was signed by curate Joseph Maye not by the rector George Hayter. I suspect he was resident elsewhere. Certainly eighty three years later St. Ewe rector William Hambly LL. B. informed the bishop that he resided "mostly at St. Hilary vicarage", (a period when about a sixth of Cornish incumbents were non resident).

There are manifest differences from the usage of St. Ewe Church today. (As a guide to my usage in this script, I state I use the term pew to indicate, at St. Ewe, a compartment seating four persons).

(a) Overall, though it is not quite complete, the plan recorded fifty eight families in 1676; today, 1990, there are twelve families regularly worshipping, most of them senior citizens. One must bear in mind the ecclesiastical parish is smaller having lost its northern part to St. Mewan.

(b) The late Norman font, now at the back of the church, south west corner, then was in the nave against the arcade pillar, the first one east of the passage between the two doors.

(c) The pulpit, now at the north end of the division between nave and chancel, then was against the external south wall of the south aisle and in front of what is now the Lady Chapel. Beside it and below it was the seat of the parish clerk, Henry Martyn.

(d) The Lady Chapel then did not exist as such but was called the "Parish Chancel" with twelve pews. now as a Lady Chapel with six pews. Transformation into a Lady Chapel, todays church treasurer, Mrs. Collins, tells me occurred as a War Memorial at the close of World War II. Before that, in her lifetime folk sat facing northwards looking towards our chancel.

*St. Ewe Church is very picturesque. It was cruciform in Norman times, the tower and spire being added in the 14th century. There are many interesting memorials and features inside, the most fascinating being the mediaeval screen, probably carved in the 15th century.*

They obviously did not face that way in 1676, and it is debatable as to which way they faced eastwards, or westwards towards the pulpit.

(e) Our chancel, then "the Parson's Chancel" was almost entirely surrounded by seating, for the parishoners, except for the parson's three pews.

We must remind ourselves that in 1564, Queen Elizabeth I had abolished stone altars, which were to be replaced by "convenient wooden communion tables", those to be placed in the middle of the chancel.The ill-fated Laud (impeached and executed 1645) ordered (he became Archbishop in 1633) the tables to be returned to the altar position at the east end, and he also specified three feet high rails ("Laudian rails"). The Long Parliament (1640-) in its struggle with King Charles I and his supporters, reversed the Laud ruling and ordered the tables back to mid-chancel position. That was part of its move to assert Parliamentary supremacy over the Church.

It looks as if St. Ewe 1676 was back to the 1564 edict, though the plan submitted to the Bishop did not show where the Communion Table was sited.

(f) what is now the Vestry (the short north transept) was then, and remained so for a long time the private pew room of the Tredenham family, its "Use maintained and repaired entirely by the barton of Tregonan" belonging solely to Sir Joseph Tredenham, knight and his heirs.

(g) in 1676 the body of the church up to the tower was filled with pews. Today the area west of the passage between the two doors is empty except for the font.

Separation by status and by sex:

This was usual at that period. "The Parish Chancel" (now our Lady Chapel) with twelve pews, six today, was a male preserve. Twenty six men are named, the "upper crust" of the parish, with Colonel Lewis Tremayne, somewhat apart from the rest as his pew was in the south east corner, seemingly unlike the rest, facing north. Also at the present Lady Chapel's altar area where the early 18th century Mohun monument now stands, the space was labelled "Seats to be erected here for William Mohun Esq. and his daughters and family" (an exception to the sex separation custom envisaged). This "upper crust" included two labelled 'Esquire' and four or five termed 'Gents'.

As the body of the church, nave and south aisle was for women, where were the rest of the men? In our Chancel, then termed "Parson's Chancel". As already mentioned, the Chancel was surrounded by seating.

In the Chancel forefront, south side, there were three pews for the Parson. Opposite three more "erected by the Parish with the Parsons consent". Where the organ now is, three pews for "the sufficientest men not placed to be placed here".
Around the rest of the Chancel, except for the door out to the Rectory and the door through the parclose into the "Parish Chancel" was seating, "for the placeing and seateing of the young men and other inhabitants of the said parish".

So, the Chancels for men, the rest of the church for women, (presumably their children too). There were three exceptions; the parson when in his pulpit, and his clerk; the Tredenham family in their private aisle; and a curious feature, where our pulpit now is and outside the Chancel area a pew for William Croft, gent, with a bigger enclosure separate and west of his for his wife and family.
Status; I have already described how the top men of the parish were in the "Parish Chancel". The four nearest to the east end of that chancel were Colonel Lewis Tremayne, Nicholas Archer, Gent. John Hicks, Gent. and John Robins, Gent. Their wives were similarly exalted, at the front of each line of pews

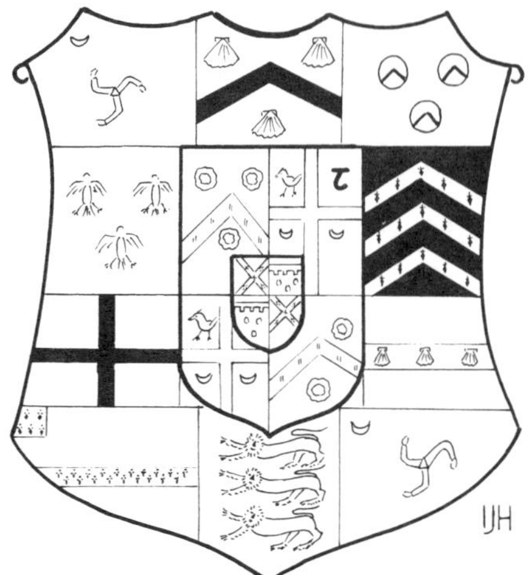

Heraldry on Tremayne Hatchment 1766 St Ewe Church

*The South aisle in St. Ewe Church contains many memorials,
and on the floor is the slate cover over the Tremayne family vault.*

in the nave and south aisle. Three of those wives, (not Mrs. Robins) were allotted pews for their servants, though well back behind their mistresses.

For the other end of the social structure, one must look at the back of the church on the plan. None now, but then twenty pews of which only the middle front two had wives names. But the front two pews nearest the north and south doors were labelled as for "the labourers wives not already seated". In the middle behind the pews named was another lable "labourers and their wives not already seated", so another departure from segregation by sex.

There remains a puzzle; the screen in 1676. Today, 1990 we have our screen across our Chancel entrance, but not our Lady Chapel's. Rood stairs, rood loft and rood have long gone. And our screen shows signs of alterations... lengthwise. Seemingly the aftermath of the Reformation hostility to screens saw moving-around but not the total destruction in so many churches. The only historical fact at our disposal is that it was once across the front of the Tregonan transept, the private pew area of the Tredenham family. It was there in 1838, when Penaluna described it as "handsomely painted and gilded, and further enriched by a great variety of armorial bearings". Possibly it returned to its present correct position as part of the 1881 J. P. St. Aubyn restoration work.

The 1676 draftsman used a double line for outside walls; his only use of a double line inside the church was for the division between the chancels and the rest of the church. Does that imply the screen, and one across the entrance to both chancels? He did not label the division as screen, but indicated that both chancels were entered by an "alley" and a "doore". That could imply a screen right across the church; alternatively something more recent, less exalted than a late medieval marvel. We are unaware when the Tredenhams "acquired" the screen for their private pew area.

Did that save it? The conclusion is; we do not know; we can only speculate. The separation of the sexes described reminds me of two experiences. Addicted in the past to enjoying the Greek Orthodox Easter (a date differing from ours) on some Greek island, I found there a double reminder of aspects of British church history. Not only was I to recall that pews for parishoners did not really arrive in Britain till the 15th century; before then benches by the wall for the infirm only, the rest standing. On Greek Lesbos, welcomed foreign visitors were also invited to the wall seats. But that Greek congregation not only stood, but men together separate from the women.

My second memory came from the English Prehistoric Society's study tour of Holland. In my free time I made for the village of Staphorst, armed with a fascinating, Sacheverell Sitwell's 'The Netherlands'(1948) which contained his long description of the aftermath of a Staphorst Sunday service when the sexes remained separate even as they went home. The women lined up garbed beautifully but identically, as if in uniform, each holding in the right hand a silver chain from which suspended a silver clasped Bible. In step they marched away, like troops off to barracks. When they departed but not before, tradition permitted the men to emerge.

Twice before in this account the 1685 death of Colonel Lewis Tremayne, deputy vice-admiral of Cornwall's south coast, has been chronicled. There is a reference in the Tremayne documents to the fact that his final years were soured by acrimonious disagreements with his son John, though I have seen no supporting evidence.

John, the builder of Tremayne Heligan II in 1692, achieved national status for he, a successful lawyer, became King's Serjeant-at-Law to King William III, and was knighted. His most publicised case was the prosecution before the House of Lords, with the King present, of Lord Mohun, a notorious "rake-hell" involved as an accomplice in a murder. So the owner of Heligan was arraigning a member of a Cornish family (Boconnoc its local seat), some of whom owned land in St. Ewe parish. And those local Mohuns were also responsible for seating planned in St. Ewe Church "Parish Chancel" close to the Tremayne seat. This space now has a monument over the tomb of William Mohun 1727.

Sir John Tremayne became M.P. for Tregony in 1690, and he applied unsuccessfully for the recordership of London in 1692. He also compiled PLACITA CORONAE, published well after his time, in 1723. He had died in 1694.

Though the owner of Heligan and the builder of the second Tremayne Heligan in 1692, he was not often resident, being busy at Court and in the Temple, and he also had a well-furnished house at Exeter. Indeed he left the supervision of his Heligan building to his mother, Mary. Doubtless he felt, even at long range, the need for a Cornish house more appropriate to his national status. The Heligan of his ancestors, built in 1603, was still in his time termed Heligan Barton, a fairly humble Cornish name.

Searching through the mass of Tremayne manuscripts in the Cornwall Record Office, I found that a university student

Christopher Hall had taken for his thesis 'The Building of Heligan House in the Parish of St. Ewe 1692-1693' So Christopher Hall had worked through a five to six year span of the four hundred year range of Tremayne manuscripts which I had studied. This thesis he completed in 1973.

Of particular interest not only to the Tremayne family and its successors but also to the local families named therein are the "Heligan House building accounts" (C.R.O. DDT.1284). They are dated between 1687 and 1693, with a few non-Heligan building details, for Sir John obviously studied and perhaps sponsored imitation or contemporary work.

For the purpose of this account, it is appropriate to ponder especially over Sir John's decision to build in brick, so unusual in Cornwall with its wealth of available stone.

Both Christopher Hall and I noted an error in Nikolaus Pevsner's Cornwall volume in the "Buildings of England" series, in which he stated that Ince Castle near Saltash is the only 17th century brick building in the county. Just in the 17th century, 1692, Heligan can share brick distinction with Ince.

One must assume that Dutch King William set off a taste for the English to build in the Netherlands brick tradition, sufficient in Sir John's mind to offset the Cornish antipathy to brick, reputably unable to cope with our West Country wet climate. Already, April 1688 John Tremayne of the Middle Temple contracted with Richard Burges, brickmaker, to supply 300,000 bricks at five shillings per 1,000 bricks.

One has to assume that Richard Burges had to be brought into Cornwall which lacked brick-making skill. The evidence also suggests that the bricks were made on Heligan land from local brick-earth. About 1989 a Heligan employee, Séan Hourgan told me, that he could identify the site not far from and to the east of the house. Unfortunately he left Heligan before showing me his theoretical site.

The second problem for the builder was to find a brick-layer. Initially John Tremayne was negotiating with Henry Godding from Bideford, Devon, but in the end the job went to George Chetwell from Mowenstow, so just in Cornwall. He was commissioned, 4th April, 1692; "That he the said George Chetwell shall build a howse with brick upon the barton of Heligan according to the dimensions following vizt, the said howse to contayne sixty ffive ffoot in length, in breadth forty five feet, and in heighte thirty five foot if the said Mary Tremayne shall think fitt to build itt soe high". Chetwell also had to ensure a stone foundation adequate for the brick building erected above it. Mrs Mary Tremayne's part was to provide on the site brick, lime, water, sand, scaffolding. The payment which Chetwell was to receive was twenty five shillings per. rod, with a bonus of twelve shillings for each chimney.

So Mary Tremayne's part in the building was far from being a token. There are a number of documents indicating her close involvement, including her careful 1687-1688 Accounts; "of what I have layd out for my son's building", items including timber, bricks, carriage and wages.

The building did not proceed with the expected vigour and speed. Site clearing and brick making was carried out 1687-88, but then there was a gap of nearly three years till spring 1692 when work went ahead, part using the 1603 building but mainly creating a new house abutting the south west wall of the old Heligan (i.e. the 1603 larder, courtyard and kitchen external wall). By February 1693 the fabric was complete: thereafter, date unknown, internal furnishing and decoration had to be undertaken.

Fascinating to the modern reader is some of the late 17th century phraseology used on the documents:

*"rudding the foundation"*

(connected with rod? measuring?)

*"paid Carpenters & Masons for Ripping ye houses"*

(ripping—demolition of parts of 1603 house?)

*"paid for six Mawns for carrying stones"*

(Mawns…baskets?)

*"150,000 'heling stones' bought"*

(heling stones-roof slates?)

"Rudding", "Ripping", "Mawns", are not listed by R. Morton Nance in his 'An English-Cornish and Cornish English Dictionary'. Can one assume those words represent late 17th century English drifting across the River Tamar? Morton Nance gives "hel" as hall, so possibly "heling stones" can be "hall stones", what we call roof slates.

(NOTE) "Maund" A large hand-basket. The word in Cornwall as elsewhere, is sometimes pronounced "mawn".

Also of interest two references to women labouring on the site. Women were paid five shillings for "carrying of stones". And again, when coal was brought in, presumably by boat to Pentewan, women received thirteen shillings and ten pence, "to carrye it up to Will Witford", carrier.

One deduces that for the building of Heligan, Pentewan was much used as a port. Indeed, though the brick-earth used was local, much material came in by sea, timber, freestone, limestone, coal and culm (culm being coal-dust used in lime-burning).

Not all the timber came by sea, for quite a lot was supplied by two local landowners, at Bodinnick and at St. Stephen. But timber dealers used at Plymouth, Looe, Penryn and Falmouth imply sea transport. Not entirely to Pentewan, for it was recorded that windows and casements, ready-made from Falmouth were landed at Mevagissey.

Arthur Edgecombe seems to have annexed the status of adviser to John Tremayne, telling him to buy culm at Pentewan rather than Plymouth, Pentewan "being nearer to Wales", and to obtain limestone from coasters which used it as ballast. He was also involved in debate wether John Tremayne should import lime or install a local lime kiln.

One necessity came from far off: glass was imported from "Stoverbridge" (Stourbridge, Worcs. between Wolverhampton and Kidderminster). Thence doubtless it travelled by River Severn barge to Bristol, onto Padstow. Thence one presumes overland to Heligan. Betimes, in the items listed, the modern reader becomes aware that brick built Heligan used some local stone. Noted in such account items as; "payd a man to search for stones 4 days at 4 shillings and a man of mine, 5 dayes with him at 3 shillings and 4 pence."

Today, 1993, as one views the Mevagissey front of Heligan, the main block, (after yet another building) is of brick. Brick on the Ground Floor ends with flat 2, with stone used beyond with flat 3 and extending to the very end of the elongated house;

i.e. stone used there pre-1692 and post-1692, except that all windows show framing in brick.

Today the viewer of the main block, of brick, must note a curious feature visible on the north side of the house, the brick of today's flats 14, 10 and half of flat 5 is not bonded into the brick of the rest of the main block. Whatever was done initially in the building of Heligan II, there were later adjustments, even possibly during the building.

One observation is relevant for historians of building techniques; the bricks specified for Heligan II were $9^3/_4$ inches by $4^1/_2$ inches by $2^3/_4$ inches, slightly bigger than those normally used in the late 17th century.

Of more general interest are the usage of the rooms. The

design, among a number, seemingly accepted (C.R.O. DDT1284/120/18) "…the draught of the house as it now is" (written on the back of the plan, but undated) has only, in the new block ground floor just three words - "Hall" and on either side of the Hall, "Parlour" and "Winter Parlour". The adjective "Winter" is nigh unreadable but has been deduced from a text reference. One wonders why two parlours and why the northerly one was chosen as "Winter Parlour".

In a trio of plans (C.R.O.DDT1284/20/5) giving ground floor, 1st floor and Garret, one glimpses Sir John's preliminary cogitations. Instead of the Parlour of the plan "as it now is", there is on this alternative, on one side of the Hall a Dining Room and beyond it a Drawing Room. On the other side of the Hall, there is instead of a "Winter Parlour", a Kitchen with a Closet, and what appears to read "Pastry" (some might interpret the word as "Pantry"). Behind this trio is labelled a Servants' Hall flanked by a passage between it and a "Buttery" into the "Parlour". On this version of the design this Parlour could have been planned as a use of part of the "Old Building", the 1603 one.

No usage names are on the plan of the first floor which has five main rooms, presumably bedrooms, and seven smaller ones.

More intriguing is the design of the Garret, for it seems to be split laterally by a Gallery, 59ft by 9ft, running across nearly the full extent of the floor. There are five small rooms (servant's bedrooms?). But the chief feature, and named, is a Library, 24ft by 17ft, with a large window looking out above the front door of the Hall.

Optimistically one can suggest that the plan of the ground floor "as it now is" (as we lack plans of what was above it) can be supplemented by the thought, the hope, that Sir John did create, for his visiting convenience, that Library in the

Garret.

One can finish this account of Heligan II, 1692, with a contemporary drawing of the main features of its front facade. It is very incomplete, being doubtless an "aide memoire" for craftsmen. It shows only three windows, none on the ground floor and just the middle three of the seven for the first floor. No garret dormer windows shown; instead over the roof is written the Tremayne motto, "Honor et Honestas".For the front door to the Hall, the entrance is shown flanked by two pillars with decorative capitals and topped by a pediment, a shallow segment of a circle in which scroll work surrounds the date 1692.

Above the first floor central three windows and part obscuring a small central portion of the roof is a pediment, the Tremayne coat-of-arms, (three right arms joined at the shoulders) flanked by decorative swags. If this feature was constructed it would have obscured the window lighting Sir John's projected library in the garret.

There is some evidence that the coat-of-arms thus used survived, but not in the form shown in the sketch. A coat-of-arms once used was rescued by being installed inside the house, underneath Heligan's cupola, on the wall at first floor level. Could this have occurred when a more modern portico in front of the entrance door was constructed? But it was not simply the Tremayne device but that device quartered with three lions passant – which I take to be the arms of Carew. And it was Sir John's father, Colonel Lewis Tremayne who married Mary Carew of Mevagissey.

That Tremayne/Carew device was taken by the late Air Marshal Sir John Tremayne not many years ago and installed on the side wall of his house at Croan, between Wadebridge and Bodmin.

# LIFE AT HELIGAN
# IN GEORGE I's REIGN

*Squire Lewis Tremayne, Born 1687, Married 1708, Died 1732.*

In the Cornwall Record Office there is a series of little Account Books kept by the young squire Lewis Tremayne, son of St. Austell's Reverand Charles Tremayne and nephew of Serjeant-at-law Sir John Tremayne. The following description, based largely on the volume 1716-1717 written eight years after Lewis's marriage to Mary Clotworthy, co-heiress of Clotworthy and Rashleigh (Devon), which added Devon properties to his tally, attempts through the limited medium of mundane details of income and expenditure to conjure up at least a shadowy glimpse of early 18th century life.

We start with an analysis of the home farm as recorded in November 1716. Of cereals, wheat was grown in three fields, Park-an-lane, (this is the Park-an-luna of the 1839 Tithe Schedule ....it lies behind the present Steward's House and Kennels), Wood Hill, and Park-an-Glasten (the 1839 Park-an-Glasson, just west of the Upper Drive cross-road): oats in Pengrugla Field (west of the Upper Drive near the present Lodge) and a strip at the bottom of Wood Hill; barley in Park-an-Loye (between Pengrugla Field and Park-an-Glasson), in Square Close and Middle Park. Lewis gave the yield by loads and the percentage works out approximately Barley 51%, Wheat 38%, Oats 11%.

Of "Quick Stuff" he listed 31 cattle, to record them in full:-

8 draught oxon, 3 feeding oxon, 1 feeding cow, 1 heifer, 2 milk cows, 5 young bullocks, 8 calfs.

106 sheep, i.e. 4 rams, 44 store ewes, 33 young sheep or lambs, 13 feeding ewes, 12 feeding wethers.

18 horses, i.e. 4 coach horses, 1 little horse, 1 old horse, 1 young black mare, 1 little grey nag, 1 little yellow horse, 1 black nag, 1 Devonshire mare, 1 sorrel colt, 1 brown bay colt, 1 last years colt, 3 this years colts, 1 grey mare.

It was a modest size farm, much of it, I guess visible from the windows of Heligan. As expected ploughing was by oxon. Note no pigs, no poultry. Was Lewis's Heligan self-sufficient? Only once did he list any purchase of bread, seven penny loaves, and one would not imagine any country property large or small without home baking. Heligan's chief grain crop, barley, points to home brewing, as does expenditure on ale yeast, two gross of corks, "a pint of girts", and sixteen shillings for the excise of malt…and bearing in mind sale of hops, and a document twenty years later referring to Heligan's Hop Garden. I cannot imagine Heligan lacking a dairy, and suggest the odd purchase of butter from aunt Mary Williams and Bridget Pascoe must have been supplementary. Sugar, of course, had to be bought, (it included loaf Sugar), but that does not rule out honey, for in his heir's time, and presumably also in Lewis's, we learn that Heligan had a Bee Park. There was a weekly buying trip, meat the main buy,

> *eg; "October 5th 1716. Marketting; Paid for part of a fore-chine of beef 10d: for a Bullock's Tongue 7d.: for a leg of Mutton 1s. for a shoulder of Mutton 11d.; for a leg of Veale 10d. for six pounds of soap 18d.; for Herrings 4d.; for three pounds of Sugar 2 shillings".*

On other occasions Lewis listed, interalia, "a belly of tripes", kidneys, "calve's chitterlings",4d, bullock's head with tongue, bullock's heels. I recall no mention of pork. Venison, woodcock, ducks, "a dish of fish" arrived from relatives and friends. Lewis's grandson, nigh a century later, had his own fishing concern, at least for pilchards, but Lewis was a purchaser of fish: he mentioned turbot, and from Mary Harris (who also supplied poultry and eggs) "three quarter of 100 Buckhorn (6s.) and other fish": to Alice Hollman he paid 16d. for oysters and 4d. for two oyster jugs, - on another occasion 3d. for 100 oysters. Dare one guess at the contraband trade with, January 11th, 1716, to young Philip Butland for 12 gallons and 3 quarts of Canary and for a Barrel of Pilchards and other things as by Bill £4-0s.-1d.? ...for the picture of a fisherman, (later he supplied some river fish) supplying both wine and pilchards seems a trifle odd. Wine was frequently purchased: sherry from James Treskowthick, red wine and cask from Ephraim Rippin (£3-19s.-0d.), 20 gallons of strong white wine with cask from Denbar of Fowey (£3-15s.-0d.), a little claret from Joan Giles, a little white Madeira.

At Heligan only two purchases of tea were recorded, both in early April 1717, seven shillings to Mr. Vallack Jr. "for Bohee Tea and a Canister", and three days later a pound of Bohee Tea from Samuel Marder. Perhaps Heligan was not yet pegged to a regular tea habit, a social custom which started back in the 17th century, and was popularised, at least in some quarters by Queen Catherine of Braganza. Half a century afterwards tea was a late evening drink at Heligan, and, nationally, afternoon tea became the vogue circa. 1840. There was one reference in the Accounts to chocolate.

Vegetables were home grown, for Lewis listed the purchase of seeds, including onion, and plants, "Hotspurr Pease", 200 coleplants and cauliflowers, 300 asparagus. There was only one reference to potatoes when he bought in April half a bushel from Nurse Halls...were they for eating or tubers for planting.

Soap, salt, spices, oranges, sun raisins, currants, broad

figs, prunes, walnuts, rice, sago, lemon biscuit, anchovies and lobsters were bought.

So was hempseed, one shilling was given for a goldfinch, Cousin John Williams's boy bought a turtle dove; Lewis paid one shilling and six pence for twelve larks. Were the larks for a lark pie, and can we suggest for the others that little Jack Tremayne had a birdcage or aviary?

For clothes one assumes some domestic activity, though only the purchase of an ivory shuttle gives us a direct hint. There was much purchase of cloth and haberdashery, and not infrequent resort to the tailor:

> e.g. *"October 26th 1716. Paid for 3 yards of Holland 10 shillings, for a yard and a half of fustian 18 pence; for a yard of silk ferreting 3 pence; for 4 yards of Galoon 8 pence; for 6 Coat Buttons 5 pence; for making a Hoop and Petticoat 2 shillings; for a skin 9 pence"*.

From Luney of St. Ewe Churchtown came gloves and leather stockings. Other gloves and stockings were bought, and for six shillings, two gauze handkerchiefs and one silk one. The Tremayne's dealt with, inter alia, tailors Anthony King and John Williams, and shoemaker Perkin. There was a little home cobbling repairs, sparrow beaks and shoemaker's thread were bought.

Not only family requirements needed attention, for family servants had to be kitted; e.g. leather breeches for Anthony White who also got a pair of shoes; for Hawkins 7 yards of canvas were needed to make him two shirts, he also had shoes.

In the months of this twelve month Account Book when the Tremaynes were at home, they needed to spend little on table and kitchen ware…two large butter pots, two yellow cups, six pewter spoons, a large bell-metal skillet, a knife and fork for son Jack, a copper tankard was mended, (doubtless a warming pan bought was also copper). Perhaps, for the history of domestic utensils, the item of pewter spoons is the most interesting, reminding us of the extensive array of table and kitchen pewter articles in the Exeter house when Lewis's uncle, Sir John died.

Briefly I was puzzled by frequent purchases of small quantities of "horse meat", till I realised this was the current phrase for horse fodder purchased when John Benallack or Thomas Pascoe rode on distant errands for the squire; to Truro, St. Columb, Fowey, Falmouth, Newlyn, Plymouth, or when housekeeper Betty Shebbeare, accompanied by Anthony White, went into Devon. Before Lewis and his wife went off for a long spell at Exeter, John Benallack's job was to ride to St. Columb "for powdering my wigg".

There were four payments for willows, and work, provided usually by Melchizedeck Jenkyn and sons – 13,400 willows and work £2.12s. On another occasion willows from Pascoe. Doubtless mawns were being made, such baskets had been extensively used during the 1692 building.

Payment of wages should help to build up a picture of Heligan life, (curiously wages were paid sometimes annually, half yearly or quarterly). Betty Shebbeare, in Lewis's 1732 Will listed as cousin and housekeeper had £4 a year; John Benallack £2 a year; Alice Hollman, or Hillman, and Philip Andrew £2.10s. a year, (the latter could be the successor to the former). The status of the last three is not defined. No wages were listed for Anthony White and William Hawkins, but as articles of clothing were bought for them and as the squire paid six pence to Mrs.Gibbs for bleeding Hawkins, the presumption is that they were perhaps, parish apprentices. There is a further puzzle:

Thomas Pascoe is not recorded except as receiving five shillings for "extraordinary wages"; at the same time Thomas Pascoe paid the squire for ploughing and harrowing; then no wages for farm workers are listed. Was Lewis's system almost a survival of the medieval arrangement with families on the estate required to work a proportion of their time on the demesne farm? It is a pity too that the Account Book listed some ten folk, including Thomas Pascoe, as paid for work done without specifying the nature of the work. Was the farm really operating on part-time labour?

Eliza Bennet came in for four days washing and scouring, paid eight pence. Mary Kittow for "wages and watching" for five weeks received six shillings and six pence; Loveday Combe, "the intended nurse" paid two shillings and six pence.

Craftsmen visiting or visited were blacksmith, farrier, cooper, carrier, joiner, glazier, carpenter, two bricklayers, "sow gelder", "old Lucas the thatcher", "John Stephens the post", two barbers, one shilling to cut Jack's hair.

The overall impression is that Lewis and Mary Tremayne kept a modest establishment in 1716-1717.

Inevitably the Account Book throws little light on the Tremaynes' social life at Heligan, and nothing on their public activities. Who visited? What did they do when they relaxed? We know that one shilling was given to three fiddlers on 21st November 1716; another fiddler came the following September. For dancing, early in January 1716, "Given to two companies of Wassail Men two shillings".

The squire liked his pipe; half a pound of tobacco cost one shilling, and perhaps he needed its comfort while totting up his expenditure meticulously recorded down to one penny items, and as he realised the time had come to pay out the land tax, just for Heligan and Higher Kestle that was £3.7s.2d. a quarter, the window tax, £1 on Heligan, the poor rate and the tithes.

For income the bulk came from rents from his tenantry, no more than a few shillings for a small tenement. There does not appear to have been a Rent Day with tenants assembling at Heligan, and in any case the Tremayne properties were far flung. For the rest one gets the impression that Lewis needed to miss no opportunity, however small, to supplement what came from rents. He got a little from toll tin, £1. 5s. from Samuel Halls, a little from tithes, he charged tenants for ploughing and harrowing for them, he sold furze; from Heligan's garden he sold pears, apples, cabbage and "other garden stuff"; from the farm, wheat, barley, hops, all usually in small amounts, though Roger Teague took 30 bushels of barley at six pounds and nine pence; of stock he sold horses, cows, oxen, in value the biggest

*Pentewan village in the background and what was Sconhoe Farm in the foreground.*
*This area is known as the Winnick and it is now a large holiday complex.*

sale was three oxen and a heifer at Grampound Fair, for £19. 8s., sheep and lambs,(sales only once topped £5). He made a little on skins, and there was one sale of wool for £6. 13s.

The most intriguing item of income came in November 1716, when Anthony Nancollas parted company with two shillings and four pence "for a trespass on the Winnick (Pentewan) by a boat and four nets": later that month Robert Gatty of Pentewan and three St. Mawes men were similarly "fined".

Quite apart from the needs of family, house and estates, Lewis had to be reasonably well-breeched, for in January 1711-12 his brother John had written to him "I have just time to tell you that you stand in Jeopardy of being Sheriffe of Cornwall, it lying between you and one Williams of Carnanton", and Lewis was appointed. Being High Sheriff was an expensive honour; indeed later there were moves to get a list of subscribers to ease the burden on the then office-holder, Lewis's son John. Sheriffs had to supply banners. John Hellier, deputy to Clarenceux, King of Arms, and Phill. Pears offered their services to design Lewis's banner, assemble a sheriff's troop with trumpeters and a butler, and kit them up in livery. Like all public office in those days, from parish constables to M.P.s, there was no pecuniary reward, and it was considered that privilege, i.e. being of the landed gentry must be balanced by public unpaid duties.

One would like to know Lewis's appearance as he progressed on official duties or rode around his tenants, but there is no portrait and we have to clothe an imaginary lay figure from Hogarth's paintings as we try to envisage the squire. We can, from the Accounts, go no further than noting he paid four pence "for liquoring my boots and spur leathers", bought pomatum and hair powder, and was careful about his wigs and cravats. We have one item about his riding style, for in March 1716 he paid one penny "for crying a pair of

Gambadoes at St. Ewe Churchtown which Gambadoes were stolen, (as I suppose, out of the stable at Heligan)".

At least a modest affluence was needed also when Mary Tremayne, and her husband, had to call in the doctors. In late December 1716 there was the intended nurse, mentioned earlier, in mid-January Mrs. Tremayne consulted Dr. Blandford, one pound one shilling and six pence, and in late January Dr. Cloke, "for his advice and attendance about Mrs. Tremayne" was paid sixteen pounds two shillings and six pence. On 8th February 1717 there was a Thanksgiving for Mrs. Tremayne. Can one assume a pregnancy? If so, the baby was still-born, as no birth at that date appears on the pedigree, (though that is not conclusive) and there is no record in this Account Book of expenditure on any child but Jack; - there had been another son, Charles, who died as an infant in 1714. From March to early May Mrs. Tremayne on six occasions consulted Dr. Seymour and Dr. Musgrave, (the Tremaynes seem to have gone the rounds of the medical profession). In four months Mary's doctoring cost Lewis £54. 16s. 6d., a large sum when compared with tenant farmers' rents and servants wages.

During this period Lewis, on his own account, had two consultation sessions with Dr. Blandford and Dr. Musgrave.

Dr. Cloke was paid for "Hungary Water, oyle of Rosemary, Julip and powders". "Sal-armoniack", rhubarb and liquorice were purchases on other occasions.

Lewis recorded payment of "Physick" from Plymouth, two shillings, so it looks as if doctors' attendances involved considerable journeying for those days: we know that Dr. Musgrave lived at Exeter.

Early in May 1717 Lewis and Mary Tremayne were getting ready for a sojourn at Exeter and Bath. They owned a coach, for soon after their marriage in 1708, Lewis was writing to a Devon cousin, (inter alia about chairs and glasses sent from

Plymouth to Fowey where his servant had failed to discover the warehouse holding them for collection). He thanked his cousin for overseeing the purchase of a coach; "I like it well but might have been better for ye countrey if plainer as I writt at first", and added that the painter had embellished it with more than the two heraldic arms he had specified, Tremayne's and Clotworthy's. One can imagine its appearance from the contemporary 1700 Trewinnard coach built for the Hawkins family and most splendidly maintained today in the County Museum at Truro. Cornish coaches were still a rarity at that date. But for their journey across the Tamar Lewis and Mary did not use their coach; on 6th May, Lewis sent Thomas Pascoe and Henry Draper to fetch Mr. Langford's "chair or horse litter", so the presumption is that Mary's health did not make her feel ready for jolting in their coach on the rough roads of the period.

They travelled through Liskeard, Lydford, Okehampton, Bow and Crediton to Exeter, and almost immediately Mary consulted Dr. Musgrave and surgeon Burns,(or Bury). In their stay of three months at Exeter there were twelve payments to Dr. Musgrave or Dr. Williams or to both doctors together, and two payments to the surgeon, (his largest fee was a guinea, so perhaps surgery was not used, or was only minor). Mary's Exeter medical fees came to fourteen pounds four shillings and six pence; Lewis also had two sessions with Dr. Musgrave.

The Tremaynes appeared to have stayed with a relative, paying "Cosen Hugh Shortridge in Full for Dyet Lodging and other things as by Bill £8.9s.4d.." How do some of their purchases fit in? - Mutton, pies, gooseberry pies, baked roll, "two jouls of sammon", cockles, shrimps, lobster, moods, sweetbreads, lambstones, "plumbs", "apricocks", hazel nuts, canary wine, a gallon of sherry, "orange chipps", "maccaroons", two ounces of coffee grounds, an ounce of

Green Tea.

There were visits to the Coffee House, three pence a time, occasionally elsewhere to the cider house, Globe Tavern, Bowling Green with Wine Cellar, and somewhere for milk and a "bisket".

They went to the Cathedral, on several occasions there were tips to the Verger, to the organ blower, and "Given to the Singing Boy who brought me the Book of Anthems…6d.". Lewis spent two shillings on a gilded prayer book for his wife. Whatever the nature of Mary Tremayne's illness, Lewis paid two shillings to the chairmen to carry her to and from Dr. Musgrave's, they had opportunities in their long stay to go shopping and to have other ploys. Lewis was bled by Mr. Collyns, five shillings, and Mary had her head shaved, one shilling. Back in February her Cornish barber had charged two shillings. This pre-requisite of an artificial coiffure, and her purchases back home of hair powder and patches, give a hint of her personal style.

They did not forget Jack; five yards of Holland 17 shillings and 6 pence to make three shirts for him; Aesop's Fables 1 shilling and 8 pence, six plain and five colour pictures, 8 pence. Lewis bothered about his wigs; he paid an old debt to Pince the wigmaker and from Thomas Summerton got a "campaign wigg" £6. 9s. He bought shoes from Hawkes, 4 shillings, and 6 pence went to Bryant "for righting my black velvet cap", purchased "two turnover cravats" with an extra 6 pence for knotting the fringe of one cravat. He bought a pair of garters for each of them, and did not forget snuff, 1 shilling per ounce. For Mary there was a new gown and petticoat from Mr.Burroughs, 6 shillings, and another set from Eliz.Russell, "a pair of Dantzick Shoes for Mrs.Tremayne and for sewing on the lace of them, 5 shillings". Silk stockings were dyed, as were two hoods, and a gown was "scoured". A new fan cost 2 shillings and 4 pence.

Household needs appeared in purchases of several parcels of china-ware for £3. 15s., (one must relate these to new table fashions), a copper saucepan,a tea-pot, a canister, a saucepan was "new tinned"; 500 pins, an inkhorn, and books "at auction" for 7 shillings and 2 pence.

In mid-August Lewis arranged with Newcomb for the hire of a coach to Bath via Honiton and Wells, (part payment in advance), a journey spread over three days. It was 8 pence for the coach and a penny for the horse as they went through the turnpike gate near Bath. At Bath again Mary went doctoring, this time consulting Dr. Bettenson. They patronised the Three Tuns Tavern, the White Hart, the Queen's Head, and "a sort of tavern over against the Queen's Head"; they went to Bengy's Coffee House every two or three days, (usually two pence or three pence each time); they expended 5 shillings on musicians, saw "the German performance" 1 shilling, were at the Playhouse 2 shillings and 6 pence twice and Powels Theatre 1 shilling once. A six week loan of books from bookseller Hammond cost 5 shillings. They paid 10 shillings and 9 pence "to the man who rents the Ball Pumps etc."; Lewis spent 2 pence "for dipping a shilling in the Bath"; he was unsuccessful in a shilling raffle for a handkerchief; they visited Mr. Prideaux's lodgings.

Normally every other day they shopped for provisions, expending on each foray between 8 shillings and 16 shillings,

> *e.g. on October 5th.*
> *white wine, a "Rabbett", tart, gerkins, capers, potatoes, bread, loin of mutton, butter, sausages, mustard, pepper, shoulder of mutton, beef suet, bacon, fowls, colewort, herbs, starch, wood, postage, silk, (total 16 shillings and a farthing).*

One notes on other days such items as six firkins of table beer (£1.10s.0d.), turnips, walnuts, oysters, wild ducks, widgeons, candles, wood, coal. As on October 10th, landlady Mrs. Tudor was paid 5 shillings and 6 pence "for dressing meat" and as on the 14th, her bill "in full for Lodgings, Coals, Dressing of Meat etc." was £9.7s.7d., the arrangement was obviously that she provided accommodation and services with the Tremaynes bringing in food and drink and even supplementing the fuel.

Despite Mary's doctoring, they seemed to have eaten well. More shopping: shoes for Lewis, 4 shillings and 6 pence; Sarah Tudor made a black silk petticoat for Mary, 2 shillings; two green purses, a little white teapot 6 pence, a neck handkerchief 3 shillings, "a little image", "30 papers of patches" 2 shillings, a pint mug, another teapot.

On 14th October, Lewis was settling up with Peter Hooper for seven weeks grazing for a horse, 14 shillings, and with barber Gervaise "for Combing and Powdering my Wigg about seven weeks and otherwise in full", 7 shillings.

Their journey back to Exeter was taken leisurely, over four days; Wells, where Lewis bought for son Jack a pair of Wells metal buckles, 1 shilling and 6 pence; Bridgewater, Taunton, Honiton. On 19th October, he paid Newcomb for the balance of the coach hire, £4.17s.6d., and John Benallack for his expenses on the ride between Bath and Exeter. The Tremaynes this time stayed a week in Exeter. Once again relatives were involved;- "Cosen Hugh Shortrudge in full for Dyet etc. £1.7s.6d.", with an extra 4 shillings and 6 pence to Mary Shortrudge for gerkins, vinegar and spice. Other cousins listed were "Cosen Betty Wood 6 pence" and "Cosen Mary Venner in full 16 shillings-6 pence". At the end of their stay they paid £5.12s.6d. to innkeeper Robert Dodge; could this be for John Benallack's accommodation?

During the week Benallack was dispatched on a journey to their properties in Chulmleigh and Winkley.

This time Mary did not see Doctors Musgrave and Williams, but surgeon Patal was paid £6. 17s. 6d., so it looks as if there had been an operation, possibly during their earlier sojourn. Mary also expended one shilling on "a sort of an oculist".

The week saw a little more shopping; yet another hoop and petticoat with a handkerchief 13 shillings, a large stone jug, a little basket, two manchets, a little image. Lewis bought a "pane of glass to the Chair", and for himself a pair of Gambadoes and some riding stockings.

They took four days to get home, via Crediton, Okehampton, Lapford, Redgate, Lostwithiel. They had been away for almost six months, but it was not till January, over two months later, that Lewis settled up with the Andrews of Trenithan near Probus for the "dyet" of son Jack and servant maid Philippa Andrew, cost of ten pounds. Lewis recorded the tip that Jack gave to Mrs. Andrew's own maid at the end of his half year stay at Trenithan.

This second twelve month Account Book, for the rest of the period it covered, up to the end of September 1718, throws more light on Heligan life, but continues to raise problems. On income; not all the Tremayne properties are recorded as paying rents, and rent payment was somewhat spasmodic in date, as indeed was sometimes Lewis's payment of his servants wages. There was certainly no sign of the custom apparent in the literature of later periods of tenants assembling at the House on quarter days to pay rents and dine with the squire: in any case with scattered properties such a system would have been impracticable. And with the small quit rents of the time again unlikely. Worth noting for speculation is the apparent absence of any rents recorded from Mary Tremayne's marriage portion,

Rashleigh Barton, unless it is hidden in items from Winkley and Chulmleigh (Rashleigh Barton's parish Wembworthy is midway between the two).

This 1717-1718 volume does reveal more of the Cornish landlord-tenant system, normally of leases for "three lives". A heriot was paid when each of the "lives" died; (heriots had settled into being money payments); for instance on 14th November 1717 John Kemp of Ladock paid Lewis a £3 heriot. The rents, quit rents were quite small, which explains in the first volume I have used of the Accounts makes Lewis appear distinctly inwealthy. By contrast the fines at the start of the three-life leases or at their renewal were heavy: witness on March 22nd 1718 Peter Davey of St. Just-in-Roseland for "the fine of a reversional lease of Carwarthen (in that parish) paid £500 plus two guineas" which he met by cash £168. 15s. 4d. and by bond £333. 6s. 8d.

It was a system really of a landlord's income proceeding by hiccups, with uncertainty for him and insecurity for the tenant, though the tenantry seem to have preferred the modest quit-rents to higher annual rents despite the massive blow of the initial fine of the "three life" tenancy. A pointer to the future came on December 5th, 1717, when Samuel Bulleid paid, per Philip Hawkins, underwriter, a £2 rack-rent on Stapdon (Devon), i.e. a short term lease without the initial fine, for through the 18th century landlords moved steadily towards short leases with higher rents but without the initial fines of the "three-life" system, though the old mode was sufficiently in evidence to be castigated by G. B. Worgan in 1811.

In this 1717-1718 Account Book extra income by sale of garden and farm produce introduces a few more items or adds details to those of the previous year; gooseberries, leaks, beans, willows, fleeces of 70 sheep and 26 lambs 5 shillings, and a number of hogsheads of "old Syder" £1 and 10 shillings each. Lewis sold £4. 10s. 0d.: worth of timber to John Whetter of St. Stephen-in-Brannel.

Now that he was back at Heligan, Lewis logged up the rents received and the expenditure on casual labour incurred during his absence and subsequently. Some casual workers had to wait for their full due, e.g. the balance to Elizabeth Bennet "on account of Weeding and other work done last summer by her and her children". Women and girls were active especially in September 1718, hop and apple picking, stone leasing. In May, Francis Slade and Dorothy Perkin did garden weeding, and there was another item for farm weeding. Dorothy Perkin was one of eight women or girls with one boy who did unspecified work in February. In July, Elizabeth Bennet and Mary Kitto came for indoor work.

Men casual workers were paid for harvesting in August 1718, and the gardening saw John May employed for a day, one shilling, in February, and Benjamin Vivian in August.

There were payments for freestone work by John Broad, stone-cutter; William Jones and John Parden for wain-scotting; John Vercoe, blacksmith, installed a pair of grates and runners in the kitchen, £2 and 7 shillings: Tristran Tregenna, cooper, "Old Lucas" the thatcher, and his man Stowe were paid. Unlike the previous Account Book, this one does record where some of the shopping was done. There were three references to Tregony, for thread, half a pound of tea (5 shillings and 6 pence) from Sibley's shop, candles from Charles Carey's; five chamber pots, six pence each. St. Austell appears twice, for worsted stockings from John Thomas's, for haberdashery from Thomas Symons's. The only other place mentioned was Exeter, Spry's for seven yards of silk. One would like to know where all the rest of the purchases were made to build up a picture of Heligan's travelling, but we must be content with logging items of interest:- "a pair of Cloggs" for Mary Tremayne, 8 pence;

Richard Mitchell supplied a dozen pewter plates, 12 shillings; Brinley, goldsmith, sold Tremayne a silver milk pot for £3-13 shillings. While at the other end of the scale Lewis paid for two wooden dishes, sixpence; - treen, pewter, china, silver, in ascending order, marked the status of table ware. Luney of St. Ewe Churchtown, who did appear in the earlier Account Book, reappears in August 1718 supplying a sheep's skin to make pockets. A shoulder of red deer was bought from the Penwarne estate. And one can add to the gardening and farming picture, by noting parsnip seed was bought and that the 200 coleplants came from Devon.

Son Jack was now nine years old and seemingly being educated away from home; December 5th,1717, "sent Jack a sort of a present to be given by Him to His Schoolmaster Mr. Symons, 10 shillings and 9 pence". And the following March, "Paid Mr. Symons Jack's contribution money towards the Victor's Feast, 1 shilling and 6 pence", and "Delivered to Jack the entrance money to be by him paid to His Dancing Master Mr. Layfield, 10 shillings". Lewis spent one penny on play things for Jack, and three pence for a spring knife. He was provided with scarlet stockings and another pair was dyed.

This year the fiddlers came later, December 26th and 28th, but the wassail men again appeared in early January.

A less festive atmosphere developed for the servants in spring and early summer. "March 25th, paid Nicholas Dabb who was then dismist from my service in full for wages £1 and 4 shillings". On 3rd June, Elizabeth Hoyte was paid 7 shillings and then dismissed; the same fate attended Mary Bennet on 25th June.

1717 had been an expensive year for Lewis, with Mary's doctoring and the six months absence at Exeter and Bath. One has to assume, after looking at the accounts of income and expenditure, that Lewis normally had a reserve of capital. He ignored, as doubtless other landowners did, the old adage "neither a borrower nor a lender be", for in the two Account Books covering the period September 1716 to September 1719, we find him borrowing from Philip Hawkins, £130: and lending £100 to his brother John Tremayne and £30 each to Humphrey Bawden and Thomas Henwood.

The farm had been without his supervisory eye during haytime and harvest in 1717, and his analysis made in January 1718 of the stock showed a drop, in cattle from 31 to 22, in sheep from 106 to 80, and there were two fewer horses. The record made at the end of September 1718 of the uses to which he put the cereal harvest gives a fuller picture of his farming operation, and we learn from it that he did have pigs and poultry. We also see the rotation system operating in the recording of the 1717 harvest, when 32 wain loads of wheat were taken from three fields not mentioned in the previous harvest, Lower Beef Park, north of the house and farm buildings on the parish boundary, and, well away from the house, Kestle Higher Downs, and Three Corner Close. Pengrugla, Square Close and Middle Close of the 1716 cropping were not used for cereals in 1717, and the demesne farm was obviously still of the unimproved, subsistence character, with presumably the inclusion of a root crop, turnip in the rotation. It looks as if each field had two or three years of cereals followed by a longer spell under grass and a season of root crops.

Worth noting is that soon after the Tremaynes returned from their long absence Lewis purchased from John Parson of Luxulyan, 99lbs of butter and a butter pot, at thirty three shillings and eight pence for the pot. Must one assume that the Heligan dairy did not function in the absence of the family?

The 1717-1718 Account Book reveals no more consultation with doctors by Mary, but in March Lewis paid a large account to apothecary Collyns, £13-16 shillings. He himself in the same month consulted Dr. Beauford, and perhaps one may relate a letter from Elizabeth Shebbeare, (addressee unspecified but one may suggest Jack Tremayne) dated 28th July, 1729, "Your papa…does not much Complaine of the Gout" to Lewis's doctoring eleven years earlier.

Three years after the Tremayne's visit to Exeter and Bath, Mary Tremayne was dead. Lewis lived another twelve years but he was still at his death in 1732 only in his mid-forties.

*Heligan is a house of considerable antiquity and of mansion size. Improved around 1830 the house took on its present Georgian appearance with two unusually elongated domestic wings to the rear, giving the back courtyard almost a Mediterranean look.*

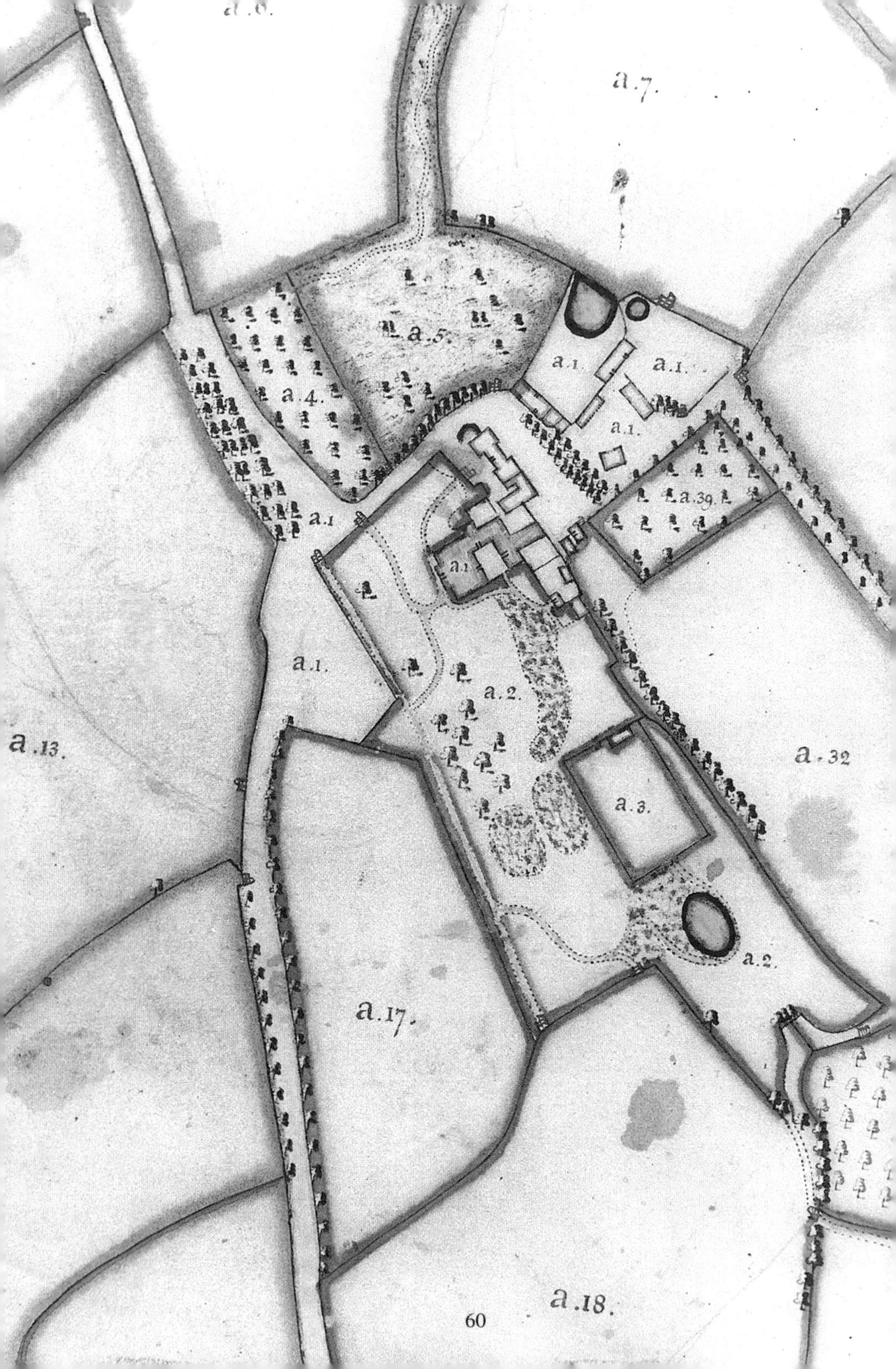

a.6.
a.7.
a.5.
a.1.
a.1.
a.1.
a.4.
a.1.
a.1.
a.39.
a.1.
a.32
a.13.
a.2.
a.3.
a.2.
a.17.
a.18.
60

# THE REVEREND
# HENRY HAWKINS TREMAYNE
## THE GREAT ACCUMULATOR
## AND BUILDER OF HELIGAN III

*Born 1741, Inherited 1766, Died 1829*

The second son of John and Grace, Henry Hawkins Tremayne was born in 1741, and Joan Giles was his wet nurse.

There survives a portrait of him as a toddler holding a whip and accompanied by a hound. Allowing for the fact that the picture, as I saw it, was in urgent need of cleaning, the unknown artist has left us an image of a far from prepossessing child.

In his early years there were two threats to the establishment. There was panic in London, with George II ready to flee to Hanover when Prince Charles Edward and his 6,000 Highlanders reached Derby in December 1745. Thomas Herring, Archbishop of York, conscious that the Hanoverian party in Scotland had done little to oppose the Jacobites, had preached a sermon in York Minster to raise the spirit of the North. Whether or not his words had the effect he desired, it cannot be denied that one factor causing the Jacobite retreat was the scanty local support Bonnie Prince Charlie received.

Two years later Thomas Herring was transferred to Canterbury where, as Primate, he had to cope with a revolution initially within the Established Church, created by the revivalist agitation of Wesley. The Archbishop, though disliking the movement -"I own I have no constitution for these frights and fervours"- maintained that controversies "more frequently exasperate than convince". Sweet reasonableness, appropriate to an age glad to be out of the politico-religious strife which at intervals had torn the nation apart since the Reformation, showed the reverse of the coin, inaction in a situation where the poor, especially in counties experiencing the Industrial Revolution, felt estranged from the Church of England.

The Archbishop's "sweet reasonableness" was to be the hallmark of Henry Hawkins Tremayne.

Cornishmen, after showing initial hostility, became strong for Wesley, notably the miners for whom the new preaching offered hope, if not in this world.

The young Tremayne was not a teenager when John Wesley first preached in St. Ewe, on August 7th 1750, seven years after his first onslaught on Cornwall…"I went to St. Ewe. There was much struggling there at first: but the two gentlemen who accasioned it are removed, one to London, the other into eternity".

John Wesley, in August, and brother Charles, in October, were in the parish in 1753, and in John's journal recorded the increasing acceptance of his message;

*August 28th 1755;"In the evening I was at St. Ewe. One or two felt the edge of God's sword and sank to the ground, and indeed it seemed as if God would suffer none to escape Him- as if he heard and answered our prayer;*
*Dart into all the melting flame Of love, and make the mountains flow"*
*September 21st 1757; "A large congregation at St. Ewe in the evening, many of whom were in Mr.Walker's societies. Some of them came from St.Columb, twelve miles off. And they did not come in vain. The flame of love ran from heart to heart, and scarce any remained unmoved".*

Meanwhile Henry Hawkins Tremayne was at "Tiverton School" (Blundell's), and in 1759 he went to Balliol, Oxford, with the intention of taking Holy Orders. It was not to be his fate to agonise as an incumbent over the growing wave of Methodism among his flock, for he never had his own parish church, and did not advance beyond the status of deacon. Instead he became not a "squarson" but a squire who happened to be an unbeneficed cleric, and, instead of totting up "souls saved" as the Methodists would have had him do, he accumulated land, so often accidentally, and in his 88 years became a leading landowner in the south-west.

One cannot say that the growth of the Tremayne estates developed against a peaceful background: the Jacobite rebellion and the Methodist upheaval of his childhood seemed to set the pattern for his life. He was to see in 1795 the formal separation of the Wesleyan Methodists from the established Church; he was to experience agitation and riot among the Cornish poor whose plight was a major cause of Wesley's success; he was to live through recurrent foreign threat and five wars; he was to hear of the revival of religious antagonism in the 1780 Gordon Riots and the agitation over Catholic Emancipation and Parliamentary Reform in his old age.

To revert to his early years: the Tremayne documents include some of his school bills, for example, a Juvenal, and Blackwall on the Classics. His first year at Balliol left a mixed bag of recorded purchases; paper, pen, ink; cap and gown; glasses, two dozen port with rum and brandy; sugar, bowls, teapot; gold rings; coal, faggots and pitch. With a B. A. in 1763, he was back at Heligan with an M. A. in 1765, when we learn that apart from his brother squire Lewis, and his sister Grace, there were six servants, Amey Hocking, Sarah Pooley, Ann Crowles, Ann Teague, Peter Olver and Jonathan John, all resident in the house. 1765 saw Grace come of age, and perhaps it was for her benefit that a hand organ had been bought in 1749 and the spinet was tuned in 1756.

As befitted many a younger son of the gentry, Henry Hawkins Tremayne became an assistant curate, in his case at Lostwithiel. But in the same year, 1766, his unmarried elder brother Lewis died, still only in his mid-twenties. So, instead of a clerical parish life, Henry became Heligan's squire and presided for 63 years over his growing acres and applied himself to the local public duties inseparable from his status.

His first addition to the Tremayne "empire" came with his 1767 marriage to Harriet Hearle, one of three sisters, co-heirs of John Hearle of Penryn, of the younger branch of a Northumberland family which had moved to Luxulyan in the 15th century. The Penryn Hearles "by judicious purchase and marriages became gentlemen and esquires" and became prominent in the affairs of the borough of Penryn.

The Tremayne-Hearle union provides a good example of the way "good marriages" helped the country gentlemen to rise in the social scale, or to stabilise themselves in the affluence they had already acquired (the Tremayne case), or even to counterbalance the effects of past extravagance. It is currently fashionable to look askance at "dynastic marriages" as if they belonged to the gentry alone, whereas one does not have to seek far for examples of poor men lifting themselves up through the good fortune of a wife with some money or a little land.

Mapping the pre-nuptial settlement, 15th October 1767, of Henry and Harriet reveals the far ranging properties of this pair. Harriet's dowry included £6,000 in public funds and properties in Penryn and twenty eight parishes mainly westward, as far as St. Just-in-Penwith. The other side of the settlement was properties to be settled by Henry on Harriet and their heirs, Heligan and other St. Ewe lands with others in twenty four Cornish parishes and ten in Devon, those in Cornwall being mainly in the triangle St. Just-in-Roseland, St. Endellion and Lanteglos. The map must not be over interpreted; it shows ownership in most of Cornwall west of Bodmin, but some of the holdings were insignificant, for Harriet's dowry items ranged from a manor to a meadow, and some were held in co-ownership. A 1756 private Act of Parliament had enabled "Madam Hearle" (widow Mary Hearle), Thomas Hearle rector of St. Michael Penkevil and John Rogers of Helston, as guardians to make leases and setts for the four daughters, still minors. Margaret died young unmarried, and one can see in the Tremayne/Hearle Settlement, Mary Hearle and her associate striving to ensure the future and fair treatment for Jane, Betty, and Harriet. The resulting co-ownership between three married couples of a number of the properties involved encourages us to expand the old saying that all Cornish gentry were cousins, for here they were tied not only by marriage but by shared land and business interests. One sees the potential for inter-family squabbles and for lawyers' pickings, though there is no evidence that the Hearle sisters and their husbands suffered in that way. Fragmentation of ownership could become a headache, if more than one generation produced co-heirs and especially if there was no son to succeed, for example, in 1759 the Tremayne lease payment to Sir John St. Aubyn for one small St. Ewe property was one-fifth of one-sixtieth.

As an addendum to Harriet's marriage, we must record that her sister Jane married Francis Rodd of Trebartha, a roman-tically-sited house to be much visited by the Heligan family. While Betty crossed the Tamar in marriage to Commodore Samuel Wallis of Stoke Damerel, notable as the man who led an expedition preliminary to Captain Cook's voyage round the world: he is said for a time to have lived at the former Tremayne home, Tremayne in St. Martin-in-Meneage. To continue the way fortune smiled on Henry Hawkins Tremayne. Seventeen years later in 1784 he inherited from his cousin Damaris Kirkham, nee.Hoblyn, the estate and mansion of Croan, a late 17th century manor house in the parish of Egloshayle, destined after a series of tenants, to be the 20th century home of the Babingtons, of whom Air Marshal Sir John Tremayne, (nee Babington) was to inherit Heligan when the male line of Tremayne ceased in 1949. So Henry Hawkins Tremayne's holdings north of Bodmin built up.

In 1808 the Devon Tremaynes petered out, and, by the will of Arthur Tremayne, Henry Hawkins Tremayne aged 67 years, inherited the mansion and estate of Sydenham in Marystow, Devon, beside the River Lyd, and just over four miles north of Collacombe in Lamerton, the original Devon home of the Tremayne branch which left St. Martin-in-Meneage in the 14th century. The Tremaynes were to use Sydenham as their alternative residence. Henry Hawkins Tremayne's son's correspondence with his father was often written there, and it was to be the home seemingly preferred by grandson John Tremayne in late Victorian times. Understandably, for it has an attractive Elizabethan E plan, a magnificent dining room with a 1656 great fireplace, a noble main staircase, Jacobean wainscotted rooms, and an elaborate Elizabethan bed in the King's Room. The Sydenham planting of Scotch fir, silver fir, spruce, pineaster were recorded in the 1823 Heligan documents, and there was much to-and-froing of workmen between the two houses.

So Henry Hawkins Tremayne reached old age, not as a beneficed country parson, as anticipated in his young days, but as the owner-squire of three mansions to which must be added the distinguished Rashleigh Barton in Wembworthy, Devon, the ancestral home of the Rashleighs which had come to his grandfather in 1708. He did not confine himself to estates falling into his lap, for he did also buy land, for example, in St. Ewe parish, Lanhadron; in Gorran parish Tregarton acquired from J. T. Coryton, and in 1792 he purchased Pentewan Manor.

King's Serjeant-at-Law Sir John Tremayne had enlarged Heligan in 1692 to emphasise his status: in like manner Henry Hawkins Tremayne, a great landowner, in the words of F. Hitchin in his 'History of Cornwall', 1824 ...Heligan, "was so enlarged and improved by the present owner as to assume the appearance of a splendid mansion".

This 1810 building work provides a documentary puzzle. The 1692 building is well documented, but the Tremayne documents in the Cornwall Record Office contain no manuscripts relating to 1810, though we are told that Air Marshal Sir John Tremayne searched for them in vain. We know that Henry Hawkins Tremayne's work was supplemented by improvement made by his son c1830, but it is impossible, without the documentation, to apportion the features of present day Heligan to which squire, Henry Hawkins Tremayne or his son John Hearle Tremayne. One letter survives, of September 1830 and therefore after Henry Hawkins Tremayne's death. It refers to ornamental plaster work, with A. Stephens at Heligan writing to the new squire at Sydenham..."the ornamental painter was here most of last week... the Paper hanger will finish tomorrow... the Scagliola man will finish tomorrow... the weather has been boisterous.... the seans are all laid up at present..."

The Memoirs of Sir John Colman Rashleigh, Bart 1772-1847, do provide one detail; he was describing the "sequacious propensity" of Cornish landowners to employ the same architect and, as a corollary, to achieve the same style of building.

*"…In like manner as Mr. Tremayne had employed
a person of the name of Dean to rebuild his house,
I followed his example, but with better luck as I
esteemit; for he employed Mr. Dean to rebuild his
house and his son has had the satisfaction of
repeating the process under Mr. Harrison,
whereas I escaped only with a moderate mulct for
a plan which Mr. Dean furnished, and suffered by
him no otherwise. A gentleman, then, upon my
dismissing Mr. Dean, of the name of Mulholland,
a pupil of Wyatt, who happened to be resident at
the time at Boconnoc in the life-time of the late
Lord Camelford furnished me gratis with a plan
which admitted of the addition it has now received
under the direction of Mr. Harrison (who has also
been employed by Messrs Tremayne, Pendarves,
Enys and others) but under the very worst
auspices and management to execute it…"*

Colman Rashleigh's final jibe seems to be at Joseph
Dingle, protege' agent advisor of Charles Rashleigh and the
subject of a future damaging lawsuit Rashleigh v Dingle.

This quote about Colman Rashleigh's building at
Prideaux, Luxulyan, serves to give Heligan III two architects,
Dean and Harrison without any plans or accounts available, in
contrast with Heligan II, 1692, where we have plans and
accounts but no architect. In H. Colvin's 'A Biographical
Dictionary of British Architects 1600-1840', Dean is not
recorded, but H. Harrison is listed as active in Cornwall 1830-
1833, a man who described himself as "brought up as a builder
and architect" (in 1840 as a builder he was bankrupted), widely
used on country houses and parsonages, town houses in
London's West End, the Guards Club in Pall Mall, and, in

Essex, Audley End's Ice House Lodge and Saffron Walden Alms Houses. At the time of his assignment for Henry Hawkins Tremayne's son, his work was characterised as of a "somewhat tame Greek Revival style". In addition to Heligan he did work in Cornwall at Carclew, Enys, Pendarves, Port Eliot and Trewarthenick.

Though it is convenient to use only the date 1810 for Heligan III we cannot specify where Dean's work ended and Harrison's began. The phrases used by topographical writers of the day seem to imply that the major work on the house was that of Dean for the Reverend Henry Hawkins Tremayne, and that John Hearle Tremayne, twenty years later, with Harrison was responsible for cosmetic improvements. Wrote author and printer W.Peneluna of Helston in 'An Historical Survey of the County of Cornwall' Vol I. 1838;

*Heligan House was first built by Sir John Tremayne about the year 1692, and it was almost totally rebuilt about the year 1810 by the Reverend Henry Hawkins Tremayne whose son J. H. Tremayne Esq. considerably improved it so that it became one of the handsomest and most commodious mansions of the county.*

*"Heligan is a remarkably handsome seat. The house, which was completed about the year 1809 is a highly respectable edifice, with three white fronts, and has all the suitable offices necessary for a grand establishment. The exterior has a noble appearance, and the interior is divided into several suites of well furnished apartments. It is situated at the head of an extensive paddock, spotted with masses of foilage, commanding the richest and most diversified views that can possibly be imagined. The whole of the grounds between the house and the town of Mevagissey (of which it commands a partial view and also of the bay beyond), are rendered delightful by their natural unevenness; deep valleys, where the rays of the sun scarcely ever penetrate, watered by purling brooks, and enlivened by cascades, by conical mountains, the surfaces of which are covered with lively plantations, adorned with temples, and rendered easy in ascent by a variety of walks that wind over the shady precipices, and afford agreeable resting places at every convenient distance".*

Peneluna does not tell us much about the house, reserving his laudatory description, rinsed with an element of exaggeration, for the view. It is our fate to use the house as it is, externally, today to suggest what was done in 1810 and c1830, for any subsequent alterations were but minor. This can be done by taking the 1692 plan alongside its current appearance.

The front building, of William and Mary period brick, was altered: the walls were heightened and the roof lifted to accommodate the 1692 garret so that the house's entrance facade took on a three storey appearance. Regrettably the 1692 pediment with its carved and painted coat-of-arms flanked by bold swags was removed. This, in sundry pieces, was used to decorate the stairwell wall at first floor level, till it was removed to become an external feature of the side wall of Croan. Another loss was the graceful doorway with its decorative tympanum and the date 1692: instead the house received a projecting pillared porch, less appealing to the eye but more convenient to family and visitors alighting from their carriages in poor weather. The local folk-lore is that a coachman who scraped his wheels against the bases of the porch pillars might be sacked.

The fact that the brickwork of the rear part of this front bloc is unbonded to the 1692 original (a fault most visible on the north wall) serves to tell us that Henry Hawkins Tremayne by 1810 extended this main part of the house backwards, tying it in closer to the 1603 Heligan I remains, so making a square of the main part of the house. The domestic quarters were pushed backwards at lower ground floor level, so that, with minor alterations, the house acquired a long narrow back courtyard, somewhat Mediterranean in appearance, ending in a flight of twenty eight steps rising to a wrought-iron gate, flanked on the north side by a slope down which barrels could be rolled.

The walling in which this gate is set carries the date 1791, which suggests that the work on Heligan III was a long drawn-out process, most of it against a background of war with France.

The result of these changes is unusual, for one is used to a late Georgian mansion with side wings at a lower elevation and with short spurs to the rear. At Heligan there are no side wings, and the rear spurs are long, and nearly half as long again as the now square main bloc. The unorthodox plan probably explains the occasional hostile assessment by Victorian critics while most of the topographical writers post-1840 ignore it: the castigations are to be found in the mid-Victorian Murray's Handbook which deemed it ugly, as did Canon Hammond's 1887 book on St. Austell, where it is treated as having been built at a low ebb in architecture. In its defence one can point out that the house, though beautifully sited to enjoy the panorama to the south east, is placed in a bowl, at least with three sides steeply rising and the seaward only sloping away down towards the valley with Heligan Mill and the outskirts of Mevagissey. When the Tremaynes in 1692 and 1810 expanded the house, they were coping with difficult levels. And surely the unorthodox plan reflects the family's desire to have as many windows as possible facing the distant Channel. So today's residents have the habit of calling the side of the house its front, as if they too accept the fact that the magical landscape to the south east – "Landscape plotted and pieced-fold, fallow and

*View of Heligan from Mevagissey, the house set in a beautiful spot*
*at the head of a small but deep valley.*

plough", a mile of triple parallel ridges, well wooded, with the cleft of Mevagissey Bay the distant accent – dictated the plan of the house.

Internally the late Georgian features are surely exempt from stricture. The re-siting of the main stairs from the south-east corner of the hall, centring them facing the entrance door, enabled the Tremaynes to create an impressive core of the main part of the house around which the chief rooms were sited. From a hall, 24ft x 22ft the stairs rise between two fluted pillars with capitals, plain except for a circlet of rosettes, gilded. The twin pillars support a beam decorated with rosettes, a popular feature throughout the house but here bolder than elsewhere. The external sides of the stairs and a cornice at first floor level have a continuous Greek key pattern. Another cornice at first floor stage has an attractive running foliage design linking small rosettes.

At first floor level the classical pillars around the square stairwell are more ornate, being topped by bold volutes above a band of acanthus-like design. Both these capital features are gilded. Between these pillars are railings of discretely decorative wrought-iron work. Panelled walls interspersed with gilded lions' heads roundels are continued up the sides of the stairwell.

At the second floor level the fluted classical pillars give way to supporting metal pillars masked by a "skin" of simulated fasces, tied together by gilded binding. Between the fasces are plain railings. The cornices at second floor level have rosettes linked by strapwork above a continuous acanthus motif.

Finally at roof level a circular glazed dome of twenty four ribs tops the rectangular stairwell, sitting on a circular panelled wall with gilded lions' heads.

From whatever vantage, from whichever floor, this

domed stairwell is a bold and eminently satisfying core of the house.

At long range, 240 miles off, it reflects, especially in the use of classical columns, the exemplar of the Prince Regent's Carlton House at least before the Prince employed a Gothickising embellisher; Carlton House, known to us only through the plates in Pyne's 'Royal Residences'. But where Carlton House, taking the classical features so popular in dozens of 18th century country houses, used them with exuberance, even vulgarity, the Tremaynes maintained restraint, even puritanically. Heligan's classical motifs in the cornices of the main rooms, hall and stairwell were applied with discretion. The applique'd wall panels were plain, unfilled with the riot of decoration which was a feature of Carclew, the home of the Lemon family. Heligan's ceilings were unadorned except for the roundels from which hung the chandeliers. Nor can we be certain that the gilding work described was original: it does not appear in late Victorian photographs.

As well as extending the house, Henry Hawkins Tremayne earlier improved the grounds. This is to be deduced from two estate maps in the Cornwall Record Office. I must state, not with the Tremayne collection but bought by the chairman of the County Records Committee at a sale of Heligan contents.

The first is a 1774 survey mapped by William Hole in 1777; A map of Plan of the Barton of Heligan and certain other tenements thereto adjoining in the Parish of St. Ewe in the County of Cornwall, it is embellished with a beautiful cartouche showing a view from the house of Mevagissey with ships at sea.

The second is undated but obviously post-1777 and pre-1810, for the house, in both maps, retains its 1692 plan: 'A Plan of Intended Alterations for Hilligan the Seate of the Rev

Mr. Tremayne,' drawn by Thomas Gray.

In 1774 the whole drive from the St. Ewe Churchtown-Gorran road ran between open fields and turned sharply to the stables, farmbuildings, and north side of the house. Today's continuation of the drive curving in a semi-circle to the front of the house did not exist; there was only a narrow lane joined by a footpath from the house. In the second map the half-circle extension is shown.

The 1774 map showed only small tree-planted areas, west, south-west, and east of the house, with shrubberies below the house. The east side of the future "Japanese Garden" and up to the Old Wood was orchard, as also in the later map.

Lacking any documentation of the planting, it is permissible to suggest that what Thomas Staniforth in 1800 saw in the Hext Restormel orchard had counterparts at Heligan - the apples Duflin, Woodcock, Gull, Red Aromatic, Newton Pippin, Red Shanked Buckland and Stubland. At Menabilly, Staniforth also saw the apple July Flower.

By 1774, the 1682/1735 formal garden around the house had gone: the landscape had moved up to the house. But Heligan had no need for a Capability Brown or Repton even if their influence was felt, (Repton did work in the County for friends of the Tremaynes) for the siting described, at the head of the valley running down to Mevagissey, had a Nature-made view needing only Tremayne tree planting. The scenic allure, with the Channel visible, appearing between the high ground on either side of the little fishing port, could bring an element of excitement as Loveday Sarah Gregor recorded in her Memoirs, when the Tremaynes watched from their windows a French fleet sailing up Channel to threaten Plymouth.

So recorded in Thomas Gray's "Intended Alterations", confirmed by the 1839 Tithe Map of St. Ewe, Henry Hawkins Tremayne, the builder of Heligan III, also created the lay-out of the pleasure grounds, as we see them today, and ready for the exotics to be planted in Victorian and Edwardian times. Gray's map showed extensive tree planting, circling the future Flora's Green and Kitchen Garden, both areas seemingly with fruit trees, and continuing on, west then south-east of the house in the direction of Heligan Mill. The verges of the Back Road, past the future Stewards house were also planted.

The walled Garden and a then half-enclosed Melon Garden, a smaller walled garden, were also on Gray's plan. So we can give those impressive features also a late 18th century date, the larger walled garden being a sub-rectangular area, approx. 250ft x 100ft, between 12ft high walls, with a central pond and its first glasshouses planned for its south-facing wall. With some adaptations it could be the Rowlandson walled garden used in his print The Gardener's Offering c1800-1805, with the gardener on his knee presenting flowers to a young woman, a scene from Bickerstaff's comic opera "Love in a Village."

The creation of a pleasure garden was not only an element designed for the gracious living of the family but a background for the social to- and fro-ing of the Tremayne social circle. Glimpses of this can be gleaned from the pocket diaries of Henry Hawkins Tremayne's sister Grace. Her portrait in oils, seen by the public at the 1979 sale of the contents of Croan Manor, reveals a somewhat severe-looking young lady, dressed with restraint in pale blue in a style far from suggesting that height of metropolitan fashion so often caricatured. Grace was married in 1776, a time when hoop petticoats were about to be deemed old-fashioned and enormous coiffures were coming in. As her portrait is half-figure only, we cannot go further than record that her bare shoulders were modestly visible and her hair-do discreet.

In 1773 one London advice was;

*"Your neck and your shoulders both naked should be,*
*Was it not for vandyke, blown with chevaux-de-frise,*

*Make your petticoats short, that a hoop eight yards wide,*
*Fay decently show how your garters are tied.*

*Hang a small bugle cap on, as big as a crown*
*Shout it off with a flower, vulgo dict, a pompoon".*

Was the portrait mentioned the one recorded in Grace's diary February 1774? "Mr. Clifford came to dinner". A few days later, "Sat for my Picture to Mr. Clifford." In the 1979 Croan sale catalogue no artist was named.

Grace's surviving four diaries, The Ladies Own Memorandum Book or Daily Pocket Journal produced by Robinson of Paternoster Row were made a feature of one chapter in Bryan Latham's "Trebartha the House by the Stream," 1971. The diary for 1774 and part of that for 1776 describe the social interweaving of the Heligan family, as they entertained their relatives, the Rodds of Trebartha, the Hawkins and the Hearle families, their friends, neighbours, business and political associates, clergy and officers of the Buffs.

At County Election time Heligan was crowded, for in those days voters had to travel to the poll from all over the county, in 1774 to Lostwithiel with the voting spread over a week. Supporters of Sir John Molesworth and Sir William Lemon flooded into the house, and many throughout the day were entertained to breakfast, or to dinner, or to evening tea-drinking, not just the gentry but freeholders travelling to the poll.

We do not know wether Grace was musical: while she was a child a hand organ had been bought and the spinet was tuned. Bryan Latham thought that a lady's withdrawing room pursuits might be behind Grace's record of sending presents, six "gold Tassils" to Mrs. Rashleigh and a blue and silver purse to Mrs. Hawkins.

Grace jotted down her travels, not easy and to us tortuously slow in the pre-Macadam days when only the main roads were being improved by Turnpike Trusts. At St. Austell Assembly Rooms Grace occasionally played cards and danced, mainly square dances, assisted no doubt by advance study and practice of new dance figures printed in her Daily Pocket Journal. She went to Mrs. Hearle's at Penryn, stayed at Trebartha with the Rodds, at Croan while, from Croan, her brother attended the Assizes at Bodmin, and, as a guest of Miss. Rodd near Plymouth, she went to an entertainment in the Assembly Rooms, walked in the Lines to listen to the Marines' Band, and saw the "Play of the Fair Quaker of Deal", with the farce of the "Irish Widow" in the evening. Later after her marriage, Grace was to see a play at the White Hart, Launceston, and to applaud the acting of Mrs. Siddons in "The Grecian Daughter" and other productions by the Siddons company at Truro. To revert to Grace's Plymouth visit, she left the port in the forenoon for Exeter, via Ivybridge, Totnes where she dined, Newton Abbot where she slept, saw something of the Exeter Races and visited Powderham Castle. In the four years of her surviving diaries, this was Grace's most ambitious journey, the nature of which can be suggested by Loveday Sarah Gregor over forty years later when she described her own journey from near Tregony to Truro, "seven weary miles, requiring four stout horses, and taking three hours".

Just as half a century before Grace's Plymouth excursion, the Tremaynes, and also the Mohuns of Luney, St. Ewe, used Plymouth for medical advice, so did Grace. She was visited at Heligan by Mr. Nicholls of Plymouth who prescribed physic; later he, and not a barber-surgeon extracted a tooth for her, and stayed to dinner and the evening tea-drinking.

Though the diaries are brief notes of a woman's world, Grace did occasionally mention her brother's activities. The odd preaching, acting as Judge's Chaplain at the Assizes, attending St. Austell Workhouse meetings and the "blowing house", and relaxing at the Bowling Club. He was also one of those involved in the Mevagissey quay project, under an Act of Parliament for completing and maintaining the pier of Mevagissey, 1775, and with the scare of invasion in 1779 he was busy with the formation of a local Volunteer Company. Henry Hawkins Tremayne was then in his mid-thirties, and Grace three years younger, and in 1776 he and his wife Harriet were busy with Grace's future. On March 24th, Charles Rashleigh drank tea with him and received his approval of the engagement of Grace and Charles. To offset one's preconceived idea that marriages of the gentry were based primarily on matters dynastic and financial, with personal affection little considered, Grace pencilled in her diary;

*"The day is come you wished so long
love picked you out among the throng."*

Charles Rashleigh, born 1747, of the family which moved from Devon to Cornwall in the early 16th century, and established a dominance in Fowey affairs, commercial, and political, was the fifth son of Jonathan Rashleigh of Menabilly. To summarise his future after marriage, he became an attorney in 1778, was three times Under-Sheriff, Recorder of St. Austell, and was active in mining. He was to add spectacularly to the local scene when, out of West Polmear, he created the attractive little port of Charlestown, with a new home for himself and Grace at Duporth. Towards the end of his life he was to become known as an ultra-Tory, but his world crashed about him in an expensive lawsuit against his protege Dingle.

In the three months of her engagement Grace listed some of her expenditure on clothes, doubtless with the help of her sister-in-law: she spent £135-11s. on the mantua maker, the milliner, the linen draper and the mercer. In May she bought furniture at the Tremough sale.

> On July 1st, 1776;
> *"I was married with the greatest prospect of happiness. Only my Brother and Sister at the Wedding. Mr. Peard officiated. Mr. Bedford and Mr. J. Pender dined, drank tea, and slept here"*.

So it was a quiet wedding, probably at the house. What is apparent in 18th century documents is that, unlike funerals, Tremayne weddings did not burden the family accounts. And in contrast with the modern disappearance for a honeymoon retreat, Mr. and Mrs. Rashleigh remained at Heligan for a fortnight receiving well-wishers, and then moved on to their St. Austell home, now the White Hart. It was the second of three Tremayne/Rashleigh links by marriage.

What Grace's diary does not reveal is that the Rev. Henry Hawkins Tremayne took Charles Rashleigh to court over a Bond of 30th March, 1776, for "£10,000 to answer certain purposes in Mr. Rashleigh's marriage settlement". In court on 11th June, Tremayne complained that Rashleigh, "hath refused and still doth refuse to pay him…the said ten thousand pounds or any part thereof". To this Rashleigh entered no defence and the judgement went to Tremayne with costs, sixty three shillings.

This was hardly a welcome curtain raiser to the imminent marriage: perhaps Grace was kept in ignorance; at least the affair was not in her diary.

The marriage settlement, finally drafted two days before Charles and Grace were wed, reveals that her dowry consisted of "several securities for Money and other personal Estates of her the said Grace Tremayne to the amount of Five Thousand Pounds and upward", to which was attached an addendum safeguarding Grace in the event of Charles dying first.

Two and a half years later Henry Hawkins Tremayne fetched Grace to Heligan as her confinement was approaching and Charles Rashleigh was away in London: a month later, on February 7th, 1779, Grace wrote in her diary,

*"I was safely delivered of my dear little Harriet at seven o'clock in the morning. Mr.Stephens came to see me at Heligan about ten o' clock in the forenoon. My brother baptized my dear child one hour after the birth."*

Baby Harriet was destined to marry in 1805 the Rev. Edward Rodd, rector of St. Just-in-Roseland and the future squire of Trebartha, in 1836, so doubling the link between Tremaynes and Rodds.

It is a Rodd diary which leads us on to one aspect of Henry Hawkins Tremayne's public life. Colonel Francis Rodd (1732-1812) made this entry on November 17th, 1784;

*"Mr. Tremayne sworn Mayor and myself Recorder of Penryn. Mayor's Dinner at R.Bodenia. 160 dined there and at other houses, cost five shillings and six pence each."*

So the Hearle dynasty through the husbands of two

Hearle sisters maintained its influence on Penryn, though neither lived there.

Henry Hawkins Tremayne was not new to the office, for in 1773, aged 32, as Mayor of Penryn he was involved with the Tinners' Riots. A meeting had been convened by the High Sheriff at the Ship Inn, Truro, on 18th February, 1773 to cope with the distress caused by stagnation in the tin and copper trade and by the high level of unemployment. A memorial was sent on 20th March to Lord North asking him to remove the duty on the export of tin which had led to undercutting in west European markets. At the February meeting it was resolved that corn should go to public market and not be exported;– "the present distress arises in some measure from the Millers and others engrossing Corn, and selling the same or meals produced therefrom at an exorbitant profit". The Secretary-at-War was also asked to send more troops.

Mayor Tremayne on 13th May wrote to Earl Cornwallis reinforcing the plea for more troops, "not less than seven companies", to be based he suggested at Truro, Penryn, Falmouth, Penzance and Wadebridge. With permission to to call up more from O. C. Plymouth if the need arose. He pointed out that the tinners were pushed toward rioting, "being daily discharged from their employments and throwing themselves, and their numerous families on the different parishes, who are now unable to support them…" To Major Steel at Padstow he explained the fears of the Penryn inhabitants at "the dreadful scene that presented itself in the late Riots when few soldiers that came to their assistance were merely for self-protection forced to do what I wish not again to mention." He described how "the tinners to the number of some hundreds surrounded and became Masters of the Town", and he feared, as corn prices were rising, that the rioters might attack the flour merchants, "and we should then feel all the miseries of a real scarcity…"

# HENRY HAWKINS TREMAYNE
## MINING, FARMING, FISHING.

The 18th century saw a series of miners' riots, and one is conscious that this Mayor's mind had interweaving and sometimes conflicting strands: he was a humane cleric who understood the desperate plight of the unemployed and the hungry; as Mayor and J.P. he had to preserve order in his borough; he was a mining "lord" and, in seeing cause to blame the government, he was at one with the rioters.

As far back as Elizabeth I's reign, the Heligan Tremaynes acquired property in the metalliferous area which was also destined to be china-clay country, but the major link with mines came when Henry Hawkins Tremayne married Harriet who brought him a share in the extensive Hearle mining interest. Close to Heligan were the survivals of pre-mining tin-streaming activity beside the river in Pentewan Valley: the Happy Union Streamworks were on the edge of the Winnick, Tremayne property. So although the home estate was just off the mining area, Henry Hawkins Tremayne and his 19th century descendants became closely involved, especially in the mines in and around St. Day, though the Tremaynes rarely appear in modern histories of Cornish mining, being peripheral to the great names of the industry.

The Tremayne documents in the Cornwall Record Office contain numerous grants of setts to mining exploiters. An older Tremayne property Trewoone Manor, on the west side of St. Austell, had brought tin dues to Henry's mother, Grace as guardian of the young squire, brother Lewis, and this holding again appeared when china clay, following Cookworthy's activities, came into the scene with the Rev. Tremayne granting a twenty one year sett to yeoman Samuel Phillips of St. Stephen-in-Brannel to prospect for china clay at a yearly rent of £15 and a payment of one shilling and three pence per ton.

Another document of an older Tremayne property, Trendeal in Ladock parish, brings to our notice a major dynasty in Cornwall's mining history, for there in 1810 Tremayne granted a sett for tin exploration to John Williams of Scorrier and Colin Harvey of Gwennap. The name of Williams constantly appears in Tremayne business papers, as it does in the mining transactions of most mining "lords" of the time. The Williamses were a remarkable family, said to have migrated to Stithians from Wales in the mid-17th century: generation after generation they showed business acumen and drive.

There was John of Burncoose, the founder of their fortunes, who, in the early 18th century, managed the Hearle mining property, the Hearles being joint owners, inter alia, of St. Day manor, and adventurers in Poldice Mine. So the Rev. Tremayne's marriage brought the Williams clan firmly into the Heligan Tremayne orbit.

The second John, who in 1748 started the County Adit to drain the mines, brought yet another link with the Tremaynes, for he managed the mining interests of the Lemons, another family involved in a rapid rise to eminence, and Henry's son John Hearle Tremayne married a Lemon daughter.

In the Rev. Tremayne's old age, John Hearle Tremayne looked after his father's mining transactions and was frequently involved in negotiations with John Williams (the third) of Scorrier, the man who leased the Trendeal sett mentioned above. All scientifically and commercially minded visitors to Cornwall knew that this John was the man to meet, not least for his collection 'the most valuable variety of mineral specimens of any house in Europe'. One would like to know how John Hearle Tremayne, an M.P. from 1806 reacted to the news tardily reported in the press that this John Williams was not only gifted in business but had psychic powers, for he dreamed of the assassination of Prime Minister Spencer Perceval in the House of Commons, hours before the news reached Cornwall.

Mining involved the "lords", (landlords), the "Adventurers" (men who financed the mines), the managers, often men in power, and the workers. The negotiations and arguments of course left out the workers, but there was no tidy demarcation between the other groups. Occasionally the system might be simple, with the lord himself the sole adventurer, risking all and taking all profits. But many properties were in co-ownership, with all the problems of keeping the partners in harmony. So too with the adventurers, a group of men, some not necessarily local, the capitalist shareholders. One man could unite in himself three functions, a manager here, an adventurer there, and having made enough money, he could purchase land and become a lord.

Not only did all these diverse and split interests have to be reconciled, there were other factors outside their control, government policy, the power exercised by the south Wales smelters, the incidence of war, the fluctuations in demand for tin and copper. There was the increasing cost as mines went deeper and needed more elaborate machinery. One can extend this list of complications: estates in the mining areas had become fragmented; the draining of one mine affected the neighbours', and one sett could strike a profitable lode only to find it reached the boundary of another sett. There were years of bread scarcity and high food prices which stirred the work force to rioting especially when there was a slump in demand for tin and copper.

Some of these factors can be seen in the Tremayne correspondence, between father and son. An 1820-1821 batch of letters can be selected as an example. John Williams (the third) and his son Michael were the driving force behind moves not only for co-operation between groups of exploiters but for amalgamation. As John Hearle Tremayne described the situation, the Wheal Jewel lode was intersected by the Wheal Maiden sett, and both led into Poldice sett. So there was a double need to get the Wheal Maiden adventurers to work the lode on friendly terms with Wheal Jewel, and to persuade Sir William Lemon to alter the southern boundary of Poldice, a famous mine with Lemon as lord and Williams as manager, for the Poldice adventurers were not working the southern part of the sett. As the younger Tremayne and Sir William Lemon were fellow M. P's and as the former was married to Caroline Lemon, the Tremaynes felt they should keep in the background of the negotiations - "I am sure anybody should take the ostensible lead in the business rather than ourselves" wrote John Hearle Tremayne.

Other letters from him showed him prepared to bring pressure on Wheal Unity adventurers so that the unexplored northern ground of that sett could be worked, preferably by John Williams from Wheal Gorland. His hope was to induce Sir William Lemon to sell some of his land.

Charles Hatchett, of a London coach-building family, who had developed a passion for mineralogy and became a F. R. S., went on a tour of British mines in 1796. On May 17th, he dined at Scorrier and described the mines involved in this Tremayne correspondence:-

*"we visited Huel Gorland which affords a rich pulverulent Copper ore very rare in copper mines in general. This ore is accompanied by quartz, green fluor and some Fluken, or a loose clayey sort of Lithomarge~perhaps this may contain some silver? Huel Jewel is also a rich Mine which affords yellow, black and red ore. Poldice has afforded both Tin and*

Wheal Gorland, linked to the County Adit in 1792, described elsewhere as a "bunchy mine", spasmodic in yield, produced a problem when the miners "struck it rich" as they were tempted to pocket specimens for sale to dealers and collectors. It was a mine which made a considerable contribution to the collection started by Philip Rashleigh in 1765, and now in the Royal Institution of Cornwall display at Truro. On one occasion Mrs. Tremayne was a donor, her son was another.

One must return to the mine workers with whose distress Henry Hawkins Tremayne had been acutely involved as Mayor of Penryn and with whose problems his own mining interests brought him into permanent contact. But it is not to be expected that the Tremayne documents in the Cornwall Record Office will reveal much of the family's thoughts about the work force of the mines, for, of their nature, they are mainly business documents. The granting of setts to prospectors, and as described 'supra', letters surviving are about negotiations. In the correspondence one appeal can be noted, for a blind tinner, George Johns. Then on June 29th, 1821, John Hearle Tremayne wrote from the House of Commons to tell his father of a scheme being mooted by John Williams that the lords, adventurers, merchants, and miners, the last 'in proportion of their wages', should together contribute to a Benefit Club. Tremayne saw some problems: contributions to a Friendly Society might be resisted by some workers long used to dependence in hard times on the parish Poor Rate; the scheme, he thought, could be really effective only if the contributions were compulsory, and he saw no chance of that, certainly not of getting it enacted by parliament. One is reminded that there already existed voluntary associations; the West Briton newspaper reported that in April 1842 at The Crown, St. Ewe, the local sick benefit club was celebrating its golden jubilee, with the landlord Edward Bice surprised that some members asked for water, being teetotallers. In that John Hearle Tremayne letter one can glimpse in the distant future the modern state compelled contributions from employer and employed.

The seeming reticence of the Tremayne papers on the miners can be balanced by repeating the observations of that exotic character William Beckford of Fonthill Abbey, who toured the mines in Gwennap parish in 1787; (re-using a quote printed by A. K. Hamilton Jenkin, doyen of Cornish mine studies);

> *"They are situated in a black desert, rendered still more doleful by the unhealthy appearance of its inhabitants. At every step one stumbles upon ladders that lead into utter darkness or funnels that exhale warm, copperous vapours. All around these openings the ore is piled up in heaps waiting for purchasers. I saw it drawn reeking out of the mine by the help of a machine called a whim, put in motion by mules, which in their turn are stimulated by impish children hanging over the poor brutes, and flogging them round without respite. This dismal scene of whims, suffering mules and hillocks of cinders extends for miles. Huge iron engines, creaking and groaning, invented by Watt, and tall*

*chimneys smoking and flaming that seem to belong to old Nicholas's abode, diversify the prospect. Two strange looking Cornish beings dressed inghostly white (the long duck coats worn by surface captains) conducted me about. These mystagogues occupy a tollerable house, with fair sash windows, where the inspectors of the mine held their meetings and regale upon beef, pudding and brandy. While I was standing at the door of this habitation, several woeful figures in tattered garments with pickaxes on their shoulders, crawled out of a dark fissure and repaired to a hovel, which I learnt was a gin shop. There they pass a few hours allotted them above ground, and drink , it is hoped, in oblivion of their subterranean existance. Piety, however, as well as gin helps to fill their leisure moments; and I was told that Wesley, who came apostolising into Cornwall a few years ago, preached in this spot to above 7,000 followers. Since this period, Methodism has made a very rapid progress, and has been of no trifling service in diverting the attention of these sons of darkness from their present condition to the glories of the life to come..."*

Beckford sets the scene in the mining area where the Tremaynes were active, but his was necessarily a superficial view, ignoring the short expectation of life among miners, accidents, disease, the bouts of unemployment, and the miners' riots which seem to have erupted every decade in the lifetime of the Rev. Henry Hawkins Tremayne. To one who has lived in the Coalbrookdale / Ironbridge area of primary Industrial Revolution, the differing outlook of 18th and early 19th century observers is startling: there was the romantic view, particularly among artists, inspired by the flames of furnaces and the belching smoke from tall chimneys; for others there was concern for the workers; for some there was glory in the way humble folk seized opportunities and rose to the industrial top; there was pride in the achievements of British mechanical genius, the inventive skills of engineers and miners. Here in the south west, whether a man was a capitalist or a worker or just a fellow Cornishman, there was the local patriotism applauding the status of Cornwall as a leading metal producer of the world. So in January 1781 Chris Gullot sent to Heligan his, One and All, or the Miners Song, of which one couplet is a more than adequate sample of its literary calibre:-

*"Lead, Copper and Tin, Boys, Huzza on our Bals!*
*Success, Sirs, to Mining-Rich Lodes and Fair Sales"*

If modern historians of Cornish mining fail to mention the Tremaynes in accounts which bring to the fore the Boscawens, Bassets, Hearles, Rashleighs, Lemons, Williamses, as well as a clutch of distinguished inventors, enough has been said to show how closely the Heligan family was tied to these dominant figures as business associates and, not seldom, as relatives. Occasionally modern scholarship provides an indirect glimpse, for example, in D. B. Barton's book 'Essays in Cornish Mining History Vol -2-', where the Tremaynes relative and partner Francis Hearle Rodd's mining activities are described – he held a quarter share in Wheal Gorland inter alia. What is certain is that mining contributed to the Tremayne growing affluence, and that John Hearle Tremayne, Henry's only son who was an M. P. from 1806 to 1825, with other south western members of parliament acted as a Westminster lobby for Cornwall's mining interests.

Notwithstanding the interest one can take in

Tremaynes' mining links, it has to be remembered that Henry Hawkins Tremayne was not primarily a mining "lord": he had an agricultural base, receiving rents from tenant farmers and developing his home farm. This must be said despite the comparative paucity of references to his farming in the surviving records. It was a period when the gentry found it convenient to have a son, especially a younger son, in Holy Orders and to place him in a parish of which the family held the advowson, or, if they lacked such, to obtain a living from relatives or friends, lay or clerical. And it suited the Church in its policy of trying to ensure that parishes had well-educated incumbents. Bearing in mind the reverse of the coin, absentee parsons, ill-paid curates, clerics if resident not over-burdened with religious duties, local history can produce an impressive list of incumbents who made significant contributions to scholarship, politics, and sport. And starting from farming the glebe, a well-heeled "gentleman parson" could be building a splendid vicarage, purchasing an estate, and taking the lead in agricultural improvement. Henry was not in this category, for he took no benefice, but he fitted well into the company of incumbents who took the lead in farming progress, men like Trist of Veryan and Walker of St. Winnow.

He became involved with the Cornish aspect of a project of the newly created Board of Agriculture, 1793, to produce for each county a survey of its farming. Quite soon, 1794, Robert Fraser's "General Review of the Agriculture of Cornwall" was in print, but the Board, in the early years of the 19th century, wishing to update the findings, entrusted a revision to G. B. Worgan of Liskeard, a most unlikely nominee. Judging from his record, a naval surgeon, farmer and inventor of new implements, (his farm failed), and later an unsuccessful schoolmaster. His 1808 preliminary draft proving unsatisfactory, the Board asked the trio, Walker, Penrose and Trist, to put

*Haypacking at Heligan. Two land girls on the left of the photograph helping out and working on the farm. (From The Ellis Collection E9272)*

*Binder at work at Heligan. (From The Ellis Collection E9267)*

it into shape. The correspondence between Tremayne and his friend the Rev. Jeremiah Trist of Veryan, shows that Worgan, collecting facts and theories from leading landowners and farmers, was using information from Heligan. Trist's notes for Worgan on the subject of woodland management utilised the experience of both Francis Gregor of Trewarthenick and Tremayne. That Henry was more than a purveyor of farming information was shown in 1810 when Worgan thanked him for kindness over domestic problems, 'my poor afflicted family'.

Obviously the Heligan estate in the parishes of St. Ewe and Mevagissey was then considered an exemplar, and Tremayne's farming status was further demonstrated when his bull won a rosette at a Cornwall show, one of the activities stemming from the birth in 1793 of the Cornwall Society for the Encouragement of Agriculture the brain-child of Sir William Molesworth backed by a widespread initial membership among the gentry, including Tremayne. It would be agreeable to know more: how did he react, for instance to the post-war slump in farming, when the Board of Agriculture, alarmed at the number of farmers going out of business, in 1816 appointed a Select Committee? Such a parliamentary device, repeated in 1819, 1820, 1821, 1833, and 1836, was to become politically popular thereafter for all sorts of national problems.

We must now turn to the third leg of Cornwall's economy, fishing. The Tremayne estate met the sea south of the St. Austell River, at Pentewan, and, as a considerable landowner in Mevagissey parish, the Rev. Tremayne was inevitably drawn into the affairs of the little port. It is said that he was directly involved in pilchard seines; the late Cyril A. Evans, an enthusiastic collector of local history, informed me that the squire traded as Henry Hawkins Tremayne & Co. pointing to Mevagissey Harbour accounts recording his payments of dues on a shipment of pilchards cured at

Portgiskey. Certainly the little cove of Portgiskey by the southern verge of the Winnick and between Pentewan and Penare Point, still with the ruins of a group of fish-cellars, was on Tremayne land, and appeared in Henry's 1767 rent book; – "Spreys cellar with ye pressing place, situated in Portgiskey Cellar Pallace and Courtledge in Portgiskey; House, cellars and courtledge behind the same in Portgiskey called Petherick cellar; Pallace, cellar and shed outside in Portgiskey called the Great Pallace."

From 1774 the Rev. Tremayne was intimately connected with moves to provide Mevagissey with a protective quay, backed by an Act of Parliament. Tremayne was an initial subscriber to the work, becoming and remaining a Harbour Trustee up to 1826. In 1803 he provided stone for the Mevagissey wharf.

An occasional letter among his papers serves to demonstrate his continuous involvement in sea-faring; For example; 1778 correspondence about the local clash between fishermen and fish-buyers; in 1792 John Knill sent him a copy of his printed diatribe on the bad reputation of Cornishmen as "wreckers".

As an important landowner with the Channel part of his boundary, as J. P. and as Deputy Lord Lieutenant 1792, Tremayne could hardly escape preoccupation with coastal defence, living as he did through a series of Anglo-French wars. For instance in 1779, when the French were supporting the colonists in the War of American Independence, sister Grace recorded in her diary that her brother and husband were active in raising a volunteer company. To Heligan came a copy of the contingency plans: in case of invasion cattle from the coastal areas were to be moved inland, those west of Fowey were to be herded back to Lostwithiel and Bodmin, while those in the Falmouth/Penryn area were to be grouped under the shelter of

Pendennis Castle. Arms were issued to the Rev. Tremayne, "140 musquetts" for the defence of the coast from Fowey to Mevagissey.

In 1782 he was concerned with the opening of a subscription to build a Man-of-War in Cornwall.

In 1796 he had correspondence about the proposal to raise a militia of 1,000 men from the miners.

In 1802-3 there was a year's peace before progressively took over France. When the preliminaries of that peace were signed, there was general rejoicing; it was reported that at Falmouth not only horses were decorated with ribbons but also cows and donkeys. But peace was but a stalemate interlude, with Britain dominating the sea and France supreme on land, and war restarted in May 1803. One of Tremayne's letters reported the installation of a battery at Mevagissey. He was to be 74 when the Napoleonic War ended, having lived through nearly half his life span in times of war.

War, had its social effects, and the impact of the Industrial Revolution, both of these affected drastically Henry's work as a J. P. Finding his law cases notebook of 1768, I was hoping to find glimpses of how he coped with folk brought before the Bench, only to discover the little book was his aide memoire especially on the problems created by the 1662 Act of Settlement and its frequent revisions which led to "guerilla warfare" between parishes, each overseer seeking to rid his parish of the upkeep of the poor who had strayed into his territory. It was a system hotly attacked by Adam Smith as brutal interference with the freedom of the individual, and Tremayne's mind must have been much exercised by a clash between, on the one side, the law and his own position as a leading rate-payer, and the compassion which should have resulted from his status as a clergyman.

As a clergyman, too, Henry Hawkins Tremayne

involved himself in education. In March 1778 the three Hearle sisters and their husbands set out to revive the Penryn Grammar School through the Hearle Trust by nominating the Rev. Thos. Beverley as master of the Free Grammar School at £20 per annum. and as assistant curate, "Afternoon Lecturer", to read prayers and preach at the parish church of Gluvias. Their joint efforts were not to last, for by 1801 the school was closed.

He had before him a Tremayne precedent for the education of the less fortunate. While a boy, before he went away to school, in 1746 Mrs. Amy Hocking was paid £7 per annum to teach not only the Tremayne children to read but also the apprentice boys at Heligan. In his 70th year he was in close alliance with the Rev. Jermmiah Trist of Veryan in the provision of parish education. There was an element there of the realisation that the Established Church in Cornwall was being shouldered out of its influence among the young by the Methodists which could be partly countered if formal education could be developed with one of its objects 'to observe and respect the teachings of the Church of England'. The contemporary debates in Parliament are salutary reading, for even the advocates of education for the poor made this proviso that the teaching should be so devised that the scholars should benefit 'while retaining their place in the social order': opponents feared the upset to society, creating discontent and enabling the hitherto illiterate to read 'seditious pamphlets and vicious books'. So both wings of opinion could subscribe to the now discarded verse of the hymn "All Things bright and beautiful":-

> *"The rich man in his castle,*
> *The poor man at his gate,*
> *God made them high and lowly,*
> *And ordered their estate."*

Looking at the attitude of these clerical educational reformers in the early years of the 19th century, one wonders how Henry viewed his son's marriage to Caroline Lemon, product of a family which had risen from humble origins to baronetcy so rapidly. Perhaps his class held that social barriers could be crossed by self-efforts but that Society should not, willynilly, assist the process. Quite apart from this, we have here the continuing process by which the Church, from medieval times onwards, fostered education until its leading role was taken over by lay benevolence and later by the State. Compulsory elementary education was to come half a century after the death of Henry Hawkins Tremayne.

So in 1811 the Church of England founded the National Society for the Education of the Children of the Poor, to counter the 1810 Royal Lancastrian Association which created non-denominational schools. In December 1811 Lord de Dunstanville chaired a meeting to form a Cornwall branch of the National Society, attended by Tremayne and his close associates Trist and Gregor. Lacking Henry's thoughts, one can quote a Trist letter to Sir Thomas Dyke Acland, which we can assume to reflect the viewpoint of Heligan's squire:- "I shall look forward to the establishment of such a school in my parish, and if I could combine a profitable and suitable employment for the children it would greatly promote the good work, for I do not want much of scholarship in an agricultural parish. Everyone should have, and read, the Bible, and there is no harm in writing, and the first principles of arithmetic – I wish for no more, but I wish at intervals to fill up the day with some habit of industry…"

The evolution of schooling in St. Ewe parish can be chronicled by three Returns made by two Rectors to the Bishop of Exeter:-

So Tremayne had followed the example of Trist, and his benevolence was followed by his son and grandson. Over half a century later, on 26th January, 1876 the St. Ewe Vestry met to

*St. Ewe Churchtown Cross, a large Gothic monument made from Pentewan stone and granite. The stepped base stone is set four square to the points of the compass, and has been used for many things over the years. The village stocks would have been placed on the platform and auctioneers used the monument during the St. Ewe Fairs.*

nominate a School Board following a government directive as
a result of Forster's 1870 Education Act, one of the measures of
Gladstone's First Ministry. A St. Ewe resolution was presented
to Henry's grandson, John Tremayne, "that this Vestry hereby
records its thanks to Mr. Tremayne for his late Father's
liberality in having so long provided this Parish and
Neighbourhood with the means of obtaining efficient
Education..." The resolution should have referred backwards
another generation to the Rev. Mr. H. H. Tremayne. The
Tremayne sponsored school, though now a private house, still
stands in the centre of St. Ewe Churchtown opposite the cross-
base, creating with the Church, the late Georgian Rectory and
The Crown the quadrilateral core of the little village.

Viewing these multifarious activities of one of
Cornwall's greater landowners, it is easy to conjure up the
image of a formidable figure, even, in our current parlance, the
equivalent of a tycoon. It is tempting to speculate this way
when we remember the lawcase, already described, against his
impending brother-in-law, and, to add that, shortly before his
death, he took to court another relative, alleging that the
construction of the Pentewan breakwater by Hawkins, which
involved changing the course of the river, was on the Tremayne
land of the Winnick, (he lost). But even while discounting the
impression by remembering the reputation of the Cornish for
resorting to lawsuits and noting that this second clash came
when Henry was old and gouty, and was relying much on his
son. We can go further and quote Loveday Sarah Gregor who
described him as 'one of the most kind hearted friends I ever
knew', and supplemented her praise with a comment that
suggests that, if she had been living in our time, she would have
approved of the American wives who allegedly manipulate
their politician husbands while remaining in the background.
Henry Hawkins Tremayne, she wrote, was...

*"most deeply attached to his wife and fully aware of her superior talents… I have always looked on Mrs. Tremayne as a pattern to wives who are united to men of less ability than themselves. So invaribly respectful was her tone in speaking of her kind partner, so cleverly did she guide him as the speaker of every sensible remark, the author of every wise resolution, that she established for him a character far beyond his merit, and my uncle a cute observer as he was, has often told me that he was completely deceived and only discovered the truth when the excellent wife was removed by her death, and her afflicted husband was deprived of his prompter. His overflowing kindness of heart rendered him the dupe of the artful, and his brother magistrates groaned over the mistaken leniency which led him to encourage those who merited punishment. Persons who were brought before him for petty thefts were sure to escape if they had the wit to profess great poverty, and after a lecture on the sin they had committed, were forgiven and rewarded with half-a-crown as an inducement not to do so any more!"*

If we accept this Gregor right-wing Tory and seemingly feminist viewpoint, the temptation is sardonically to employ the phraseology of the pulpit, suggesting that this owner of broad acres was an example of "the meek inheriting the earth".

Regrettably Harriet Tremayne rarely appears in the surviving Tremayne documents, but we learn that her health failed for some years before her death in 1805 and that a stroke had crippled her. Sarah Gregor said that she was 'well informed for her time': she was one of the ladies involved in 1791 in the creation of the Powder Book Club, 'the earliest of its kind in

Cornwall'. Twelve ladies; Harriet, Sarah Gregor's aunt Mrs. Gregor, and Mrs. Carlyon of Tregrehan, these were among the initial members: they met in Tregony and once a year dined together. They had a male secretary the Rev. Jeremiah Trist and one suspects that formidable censor of books bossed the arrangements - it is recorded that he used scissors and the study fire on one of his own volumes, that 'profligate and immoral book' Pierre Boyle's Dictionaire Historique et Critique. History, Travels, Biography, politics, Belles Letters were to be their range, advised of course by Trist, with an annual subscription of one guinea used to buy the members choice of book. After adequate use, the members could purchase club books at half cost price. Sarah Gregor's assessment was that, in days when the ladies were separated by distance and inferior roads, the Club 'contributed in many ways to the improvement of society'. One can almost dub the Powder Book Club as a group of Cornish blue-stockings. Christine North (County Archivist), who rescued the Club from oblivion in her study of the Trists, has cited four books read: Gisbourne's Duties of Women, The Works of Sir Joshua Reynolds, A Survey of Turkey, Pratt's Gleanings – hardly light reading.

To the late Cyril A. Evans I owe this description of the portrait of Harriet and her husband which he saw in the Library of Heligan, before the house was vacated;

*"He is shown in quiet clerical attire, black. His hair white, and curled in a broad wave below the line of the hat, much resembling Charles Wesley. He is standing at a table placed by the window of the same room at Heligan in which the picture was then hung, and, apart from the way in which the heavy curtains are looped up, there is hardly any difference in the room to what it was when the picture was painted. His hand is on a small telescope, mounted on a stand.*

*Heligan Mill ~ Generations of Mevagissey families have walked the many paths through the woods to the 400 year old grist mill situated in the valley below Heligan House.*

# POST-HELIGAN III
## 19th CENTURY

In 1829 the Reverend Henry Hawkins Tremayne, builder of Heligan III, died. He was succeeded by John Hearle Tremayne, born 1780, and who, in 1813 married Caroline Matilda Lemon, daughter of Sir William Lemon of Carclew. John Hearle Tremayne already in his father's life-time was involved in other than purely local affairs, for he was in the House of Commons 1806-1825 as M.P. for Cornwall.

When John Hearle Tremayne died in 1851 he was succeeded by John Tremayne, also a Cornwall M.P., and a squire who ruled over Heligan for a long spell, 1851-1901. In 1860 he married the Hon. Mary Charlotte Crespigny, eldest daughter of the 2nd Baron Vivian of Glynn. Hence another celebratory heraldic plaque was added to the late 15th century screen in St. Ewe Church. And a stained glass window in its south aisle laments the death in 1867 of his first baby Perys.

It was in the tail-end of his father's regime and in the early years of his own that John Tremayne's mind, quite apart from his involvement in national politics, had to embrace international concepts. I select two examples, in the following chapters, to demonstrate that Heligan and its Tremayne family had a non-local involvement. Firstly I record John's brother Arthur as a Dragoon in the Crimean War, and secondly, John's inherited fostering in Heligan's grounds of botanical treasures, rhododendrons, from distant lands.

Not so distant as the Crimea or the rhododendron world of Nepal, to me, (and at Cambridge I was a rowing man), it is worth recording that Henry Hawkins Tremayne, third son of John Hearle Tremayne, was in the Oxford boat in March 1849, rowing on the bow side at three, weighing eleven stone five pounds. The Cambridge crew, all from Trinity, were fitter and from Chiswick Eyot left the Oxford boat trailing sadly.

But 1849 had a special place in the rowing annals for Oxford, stung by their defeat, challenged Cambridge to a second race, which took place in December. On that occasion four of the Oxford crew were changed, and Tremayne was one of those left out. Cambridge won, just, but the umpire gave the race to Oxford, alleging a Cambridge foul for crossing over into Oxford's water.

As an addendum I record what I was told by Patrick Strong at Eton, checking the 19th century Eton Registers where he noted six Tremaynes;

| | | |
|---|---|---|
| *John,* | *eldest son of* *John Hearle Tremayne, Eton* | *1838~1842* |
| *Arthur,* | *second son* | *1839~1845* |
| *Henry Hawkins,* | *Third son* | *1841~1848* |
| *William Francis,* | *second son of Lt.Col.Arthur* *Tremayne of Carclew* | *1876~1878* |
| *John Hearle,* | *fourth son* | *1879~1883* |
| *John Claude Lewis,* | *only son of John Tremayne* *of Heligan* | *1883~1884* |

# ARTHUR TREMAYNE
## IN THE CAVALRY.

In 1844 John Hearle Tremayne addressed himself at Heligan, to the problem of a military career for his second son, Arthur, then at Eton and having completed his seventeenth year. Back from the Horse Guards came the reply that Arthur's had been added to the names of candidates for a cornetcy by purchase, but Lt. General Lord Fitzroy Somerset sent on the Duke of Wellington's warning that there would be a considerable delay as there was already a waiting list.

In the spring and summer of 1846 matters were stirring and the Heligan Tremaynes were receiving advice from Hearle-Stephens stationed in Ireland as to the choice of regiment:-

17th Lancers and 7th Hussars "both very nice", 8th Hussars "a very slow set", 16th Lancers "a very distinguished Corps as will be on their return one of the most crack Regiments", 11th Hussars "I would not put a youngster into that Corps. As no one seems able to get on with Lord Cardigan", 13th Light Dragoons "a very nice Corps and under a very good commanding officer". A second letter dealt with the Heavy Brigade:- "1st Royal Dragoons, Scots Greys, and 6th Iniskilling, I do not like them."

On the 11th September, 1846 Arthur was commissioned - a cornetcy by purchase in the 13th Light Dragoons. Hearle Stephens was giving advice on uniform and chargers, Arthur's sword was being purchased from Wilkinson in Pall Mall, a vet was assessing a chestnut gelding, and another correspondent was advising Arthur would need a servant as well as a batman. For the next three years Arthur, stationed in Ireland, created problems. Keeping up with the cavalry Joneses and soon desiring promotion, by purchase, he wrote letters home with a constant financial thread... "a man without a gun seems like a fox without a brush"… "I collected my bills before leaving Dublin… I know how foolish and extravagant I have been", October 1847. In the same month Felton Harvey, stationed at Mullingar, wrote to John Hearle Tremayne about purchasing a lieutenant for Arthur, a matter of £2,000 – "I suppose you are aware that the Horse Guards do not recognise anything above regulations and in any communication which you may have with any Army official nothing must be said about the extra sum…"

Two months later Arthur, doubtless under pressure from his father was listing his expenses, furnishing his rooms, batman, livery. In November 1850 Arthur was still making excuses and promises – "I will in future try, and will lead a less extravagant life". In 1851, stationed in Scotland, he was wheedling father to purchase a captaincy for him. In March he reviewed the impact on his expenses of a rise in rank:- £39 on being gazetted; "on becoming a Captain my third horse is put on the diary as a charger"… "my pay will be 14 shillings and 7 pence per diem. I think that is about £266 and 10 shillings a year. As a lieutenant it has been 9 shillings per diem or about £164 a year". So pre-occupied when he wrote home with his personal affairs, the young Tremayne's letters only just managed to hint at the fact that he had arrived in Ireland in the middle of the Great Famine, for the potato blight, having earlier appeared in England, spread to Ireland in the Autumn of 1845 and did not peter out till 1848 – "the worst event of its kind recorded in European history at a time of peace."

The 13th Light Dragoons were part of the British forces engaged in the Crimean War. Every schoolboy has heard of the Charge of the Light Brigade: there is no need for me to retell the story, a tragedy occasioned by poor Captain Nolan's misunderstanding of the orders he had been given by Lord Raglan to convey to Lord Lucan. As for Arthur Tremayne, the first line in the Charge behind Lord Cardigan consisted of the 17th Lancers and Arthur's 13th Light Dragoons. It was a bloody episode. Nearly seven hundred men were involved. Three hundred and thirty five Light Brigade horses were killed. Of the nigh seven hundred men, two hundred and seventy eight were wounded, missing or killed. In the whole of the Battle for Balaclava those Charge losses accounted for well over a third.

When the officers received the London newspapers, they read how Lord Cardigan had been feted at the Mansion House. One penned his comments on what he read; he recorded the merriment of his fellow officers and added "I never read a more egotistical speech in my life, to say nothing of the wonderful way in which Lord Cardigan indulges his imagination". Despite our understandable national desire to acclaim our men involved in military disaster, Lord Cardigan soon lost the temporary adulation expressed, and reverted to his so frequent state of being without esteem.

The Charge of the Light Brigade was on October 15th, 1854. The Crimean War ended in 1856. Two years later Arthur Tremayne married Lady Francis Hely-Hutchinson. She died in 1866, mother of four children. In 1869 Arthur inherited Carclew from his maternal uncle, Sir Charles Lemon. In 1870 Arthur married again, to Emma, daughter of the Reverend Thomas Phillpotts of Porthgwidden, St. Ives

FOOTNOTE. (From I.J.HERRING)
Deene Park, Northamptonshire, home of Lord Cardigan, is but ten miles from my boyhood home. My maternal grandfather knew him. And I have treasured for some years a kind present from Lord Cardigan's descendant, a colour transparency of the oil painting of Lord Cardigan on his famous charger.
I also have installed on my bedroom wall, an 1863 Ackerman print "The Light Dragoons".
(The Cornwall Record Office manuscripts used in the above are; DDT 2884, 2885, 2887, 2888, 2889, 2891, 2893-2899, 2901.)

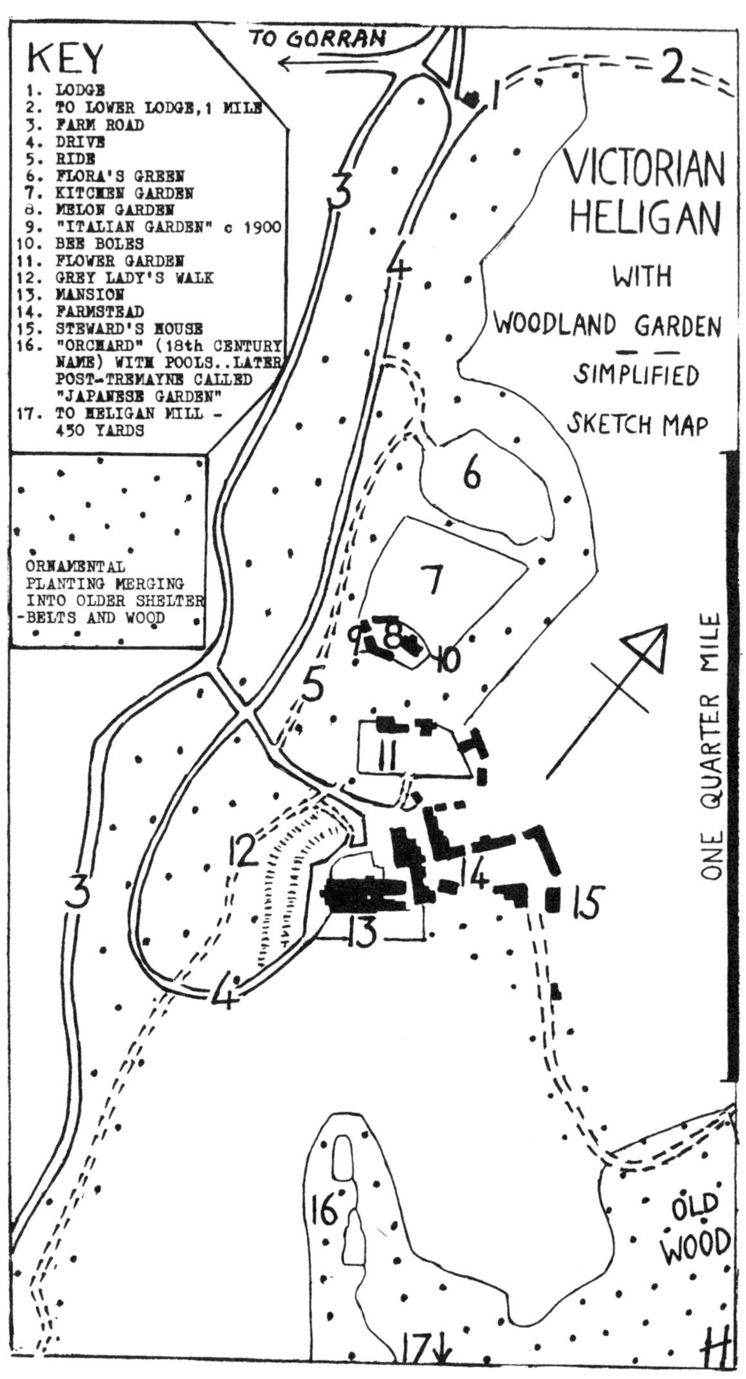

KEY
1. LODGE
2. TO LOWER LODGE, 1 MILE
3. FARM ROAD
4. DRIVE
5. RIDE
6. FLORA'S GREEN
7. KITCHEN GARDEN
8. MELON GARDEN
9. "ITALIAN GARDEN" c 1900
10. BEE BOLES
11. FLOWER GARDEN
12. GREY LADY'S WALK
13. MANSION
14. FARMSTEAD
15. STEWARD'S HOUSE
16. "ORCHARD" (18th CENTURY NAME) WITH POOLS..LATER POST-TREMAYNE CALLED "JAPANESE GARDEN"
17. TO HELIGAN MILL - 450 YARDS
ORNAMENTAL PLANTING MERGING INTO OLDER SHELTER -BELTS AND WOOD
TO GORRAN
VICTORIAN HELIGAN
WITH
WOODLAND GARDEN
—
SIMPLIFIED
SKETCH MAP
ONE QUARTER MILE
OLD WOOD

# HOOKER; BENEFACTOR OF CORNISH GARDENS, INCLUDING HELIGAN.

Heligan's long woodland garden is not just a local creation. Behind it were international ventures. Important in Heligan's achievement is the extensive planting of rhododendrons. So behind Heligan is Nepal and the work there of Joseph Hooker.

It is so easy to slip into an insular outlook, enjoying the rhododendrons in our woodland gardens acclaimed botanical residents of Britain for 130 years, and in some cases longer, as if they were natural to our scene. So it is good, when incarcerated by the gales upending nature, trees, and blowing planted layers out of the ground, to remind ourselves, through contemporary journals, of those intrepid plant collectors of yesteryear, and to see, through their eyes, the distant native habitats of our treasures.

In March 1984 a co-resident of Heligan, took from her shelves to lend me Sir Joseph Hooker's "Himalayan Journals", the 1891 reprint revised by the author from the original 1854 edition. She, Mrs. Joan Henkel, as a small girl lived in Nepal, and, to honour her, I had planted near her then favourite woodland pitch a 'Cornus capitata', once the glory of Heligan, the first garden in Britain to grow it from seeds given by Sir Antony Buller to J. H. Tremayne in 1825.

I began to read the journal alongside a list of rhododendrons noted at Heligan by observers between 1897 and 1950, cumulatively including some twenty Hooker importations.

Hooker's journal is absorbing, not merely for his botanical and scientific observations, but for a wealth of verbal vignettes of the customs of the many people among whom he travelled across the Plains of India up to Darjeeling, his base for exploring Nepal and Sikkim. The journals rapidly removed my misconception of a plant collector aided by a small compact group of assistants: Hooker, as he moved into Nepal had a party of fifty six, and he listed the impressive amount of gear carried. Throughout one senses the immense difficulties of the terrain, varying from sub-tropical valleys up to mountain snows. As one reads his botanical descriptions, it is difficult not to query the repeated appraisal of Cornish rhododendrons as finer and taller than their Himalayan parents.

Is this just flattery or blanket assessment? Hooker certainly recorded in the Himalayans 'R. argenteum(grande) as 40ft high and R.Falconeri 40-50ft tall.'

Cornish rhododendrons grow cheek by jowl at lowly elevations so that it is interesting to compare Hooker's altitude observations, for example, "at the resting-house of Laghep, alt. 10,475ft, where he spent two days gathering rhododendron seed below and above his camp". Not infrequently the names allotted by Hooker to his finds commemorated people who assisted him, examples from the Heligan lists are, R. Aucklandii, Campbelli, Dalhousiae, Falconeri, and Hodgsoni.

Joseph Hooker brought back from Sikkim, Himalayas, between, 1847-1850, forty five new rhododendron species. In her book "Rhododendrons and Azaleas," published by Faber 1964, Judith Berresford listed sixteen species of seeds which reached his friends and acquaintances who had gardens in suitable places, and in Cornwall that would have been, Carclew and Penjerrick.

From Carclew, Heligan benefited.

Judith Berresford's list:

| Rhododendron | griffithianum | lanatum |
| | campylocarpum | glaucophyllum |
| | wightii | lepidotum |
| | thomsonii | edgwortii |
| | falconeri | barbatum |
| | grande | |
| | maddenii | |
| | fulgens | |
| | niveum | |
| | hodgsonii | |
| | wallichii | |

*Heligan House at about 1900, photographed by H. D. Wootton of Redruth.
It has changed very little. The house achieved this appearance in 1810 when the
1692 house was enlarged by the Reverend Henry Hawkins Tremayne.*

*Heligan House with what looks like a garden party taking place.
The date of the photograph is unknown.*

*Heligan House as it is today. Divided into 22 flats, the residents
having formed a company have bought up the freehold of the house.*

# HELIGAN IN THE 20th CENTURY

As this chronicle approaches the 20th century, one is conscious that we, in the 1890s, were at the end of an era. We had reached the final years of Queen Victoria's long reign, and, locally, Heligan was in the last years of the squirearchy of John Tremayne... a long spell. The Queen and John Tremayne both died in 1901. And John Tremayne's only surviving son, John Claude Lewis Tremayne, born 1869, was to be the last owner of Heligan in direct line of succession, for after him inherited a nephew, John, son of Charles Babington who in 1889 had married Grace Damaris Matilda Tremayne. That John was destined to be Heligan's owner as Air Marshal Sir John who converted the house into flats in the early 1970's.

Yet though change was dominant, the ecclesiastical parish of St. Ewe produced in the late 1890s aspects familiar to us today. In the 1980s the Anglican parishes of St. Ewe and Mevagissey were merged with the Vicar of Mevagissey becoming also the Rector of St. Ewe. I select the St. Austell Deanery Magazine of 1897 to show that the two churches, though not then officially united, betimes merged in combined activities, sponsored by the Tremaynes of Heligan. On July 15th, 1897, a Joint Bazaar was held at Heligan by invitation of the Hon. Mrs. Tremayne. It was recorded that nearly 2,000 people were present, appreciating the beautiful grounds in fine weather. Special thanks were voiced to Mrs. Tremayne and her daughters not only for lending the grounds but for their "service, warm interest and assiduous labours".

After our own long years of inflation, it is intriguing to read the financial result of that 1897 well-attended function: the gross proceeds were £223, and the balance, after meeting costs, £193, allotted as follows; to St. Ewe Church £111,

Mevagissey Church £82. The Magazine recorded that the St. Ewe stall took £43, the Mevagissey stall £21.

This joint Bazaar was no rare occasion for the two parishes involved together at Heligan. And the Heligan lady did more than decorate the church, help with refreshments and head subscription lists on routine occasions. I cite two: firstly December 29th, 1896, a Concert and Farce in the Mevagissey Board School Room was under the patronage of the Hon. Mrs. Tremayne, its proceeds were to go to the building fund of the Church School; secondly in 1899 to swell the building fund for the Public Rooms in Mevagissey, folk planned for Heligan a Nautical Fancy Fair to be opened by John Claude Tremayne. I can only suggest that the Second Boer War 1899-1902 preoccupied minds to the exclusion of local more peaceful interests.

Lest the impression be given that Heligan ladies dominated St. Ewe-Mevagissey ecclesiastical friendship, I recall that at one stage both churches had a Tremayne church-warden. I cannot cite documentary proof, but the 1897 St. Austell Deanary Magazine noted that at the Easter Vestry John Claude Tremayne resigned his Mevagissey churchwarden post, the family was not pegged to its parish church of St. Ewe. It is now appropriate to record some facts about John Claude Tremayne, the last Tremayne to inherit Heligan indirect line of succession. He was born in 1869, and died in Italy in 1949. Kelly's Handbook to the Titled, Landed, and Official Classes (1929) reveals; J. C. L. Tremayne was educated at Eton and was to be involved in the militia as Captain in the 3rd Battalion the Duke of Cornwall's Light Infantry, 1894, and 1900-02, and again from 1914. He became a J. P. and in 1918 was awarded the O. B. E.

I note in the literature stemming from the National Trust that John Claude, in his late 60's, ran into trouble, facing an outcry, supported by The Times, about his desire in 1936 to develop the Rumps, the beauty spot on the North Coast of Cornwall. He put 360 acres on the market, divided into proposed building plots. Eventually the vigorous opposition was rewarded when the area was bought by the National Trust. Twenty years earlier John Claude appeared in the Cornish press more favourably when it recorded that, at the 1911 Royal Cornwall Agricultural Association show at St. Austell, he won four awards in the Jersey cattle classes and in addition gained a special prize for the best Jersey cow and heifer milk. The next year Heligan's farm gained four more Jersey awards at the show held at Penzance.

The records suggest that in his old age John Claude preferred to live at his other house, Boccanegra Ventimiglia, an attractive coastal site between Monaco and San Remo, so very close to the Franco-Italian border. It was previously owned by Ellen Willmott 1905-1923: John Claude bought it in 1923, ten years before her death in 1934. Discovery of this fact impinged on me as one of a number of coincidences linking my past with my Heligan present. For many years I lived on the Essex fringe of London, not far, fourteen miles, from the site of Ellen Willmott's house and famous garden, Warley Place near Brentwood. It was a house demolished just before World War II, and I wandered through its garden relapsed into the wild during the 1960s. Because her great book, 'The Genus Rosa' (Murray 1910-1914) helped to turn me into a modest collector of Old-Fashioned Roses, I put together her story, and my illustrated article 'The Great Gardener of Great Warley' which was published in 'The Essex Countryside Vol. 18', November 1969. I found her a fascinating personality as well as a great gardener. One who betimes was hostess to Queen Mary at Great Warley and her companion at rose shows. Now, 1993, I was writing of a Tremayne who acquired Ellen Willmott's

Boccanegra, and, concurrently I encountered an account 'Boccanegra, a Riviera garden' by Audrey le Lievre, and a book by Penelope Tremayne 'Under Helicon' (1987) containing a section on Boccanegra.

Let us now turn to John Claude Lewis Tremayne's successor, Air Marshal Sir John Tremayne, born 1891, died 1979. He was born a Babington, his father Charles Babington having married Grace Tremayne, sister of John Claude Lewis Tremayne. He changed his surname to Tremayne in 1945, some say when he inherited from John Claude, but, as John Claude did not die till 1949, that idea poses problems. Others say he altered his name on deciding to settle down in Cornwall. Perhaps in 1945 he already knew he was to inherit Heligan, a possibility which can eliminate my puzzlement.

He was a most distinguished airman, initially with the Naval wing of the Royal Flying Corps, but later with the R. A. F. Aged 23, he was spectacularly involved three and a half months after the German invasion of Belgium began World War I. John Babington was one of three pilots ordered to raid the Zeppelin sheds at Freidrichshafen, described by one historian as a flight of 250 miles into gun-fire, across enemy country, in the frail little Avro with its humble horse power, an achievement with the best of them. It was an auspicious start to a top-level career.

Between the two World Wars his status rocketed, not only within the R. A. F. but as representative on preparatory disarmament work and at the Geneva Conference. The eve of World War II found him, an Air Vice-Marshal at Singapore, Air Officer Commanding for the Far East, and already since 1934 a C. B. E.

At Singapore he was in the debate over the expected outbreak of war with Japanese involvement, as to which route aimed at Singapore a hostile army would take. He also supported moves to replace overall army dominance of planning by a Defence Committee including all three Services. So, when war began, 1939, the Far East Defence Committee became its War Committee, headed by the Governor with his top civil servant and the heads of all three Services. Major General Woodburn Kirby, author of the book on the war against Japan, recorded clashes between Air Marshal Babington and Major General L. V. Bond, and of behind the scenes manoeuvring which led to both men being replaced in the spring of 1941.

Babington back in England was kept busy as Commander-in-chief Technical Training. He was awarded the K. C. B. and in 1943 headed the R. A. F. mission to Moscow.

In 1944, his 53rd year, he retired from the R. A. F. and entered civilian life. Cornwall found him work to do as Deputy Lord Lieutenant in 1945 and as High Sheriff in 1954, a local involvement saddened by the death in 1954 of Lady Tremayne. Air Marshal Sir John Tremayne having inherited Heligan in 1949 was faced by a problem not infrequent in the second half of the 20th century when mansions of yesteryear, over spacious and needing a sizeable domestic staff, ceased to fit the social and economic condition of Great Britain.

Sir John already inhabited another Tremayne house Croan appreciatively described by A. L. Rowse in his Memories of Men and Women, published 1980. A. L. Rowse, Sir John's luncheon guest together with Princess Marthe Bibesco wrote :-

*"One last Cornish trip, from my Journal, to beautiful Croan, near Wadebridge, a William and Mary manor-house which the taste of an Air Marshal, Sir John Tremayne, had made still more so. The square farmyard beside the house he had turned into a formal court, rather Italianate, with urns and summer houses. Within, the house was haunted by a Queen*

*Anne lady, Madam Damaris, whose portrait hung in the drawing room; tapestry furniture, petit point, "the house smells like Hatfield", as one of the Cecils said, - that nostalgic fragrance of polished wood, beeswax and wood-smoke which David Cecil describes in his book about Hatfield."*

In 1978 shortly after I came to Heligan, I met Sir John who reminisced about the past centuries of the house, he knowing that I, a historian, was busy with the Tremayne manuscripts in the Cornwall Record Office. After his death I went to the Croan sale where I noticed on the side-wall of the house the Tremayne coat-of-arms, a carving originally part of Heligan's facade. I also recognised, from an old photograph I had, that the urns in Croan's formal court had once been flanking Heligan's forecourt. And among my photocopies of Heligan drawings by G. H. Kitchen, (in the Collection of the Royal Institute of British Architects), I have one of a splendid gate to Heligan's walled garden... a gate now at Croan.

So what could Sir John do with Heligan? What did his predecessor do with it when he preferred to live at Boccanegra? – he found tenants for the house. In 1929 the Williamsons, (New Zealanders) and after them, Commander Thomas, c1947 or later.

Of course two World Wars temporarily imposed solutions. In 1914-1918 War the house was used for convalescing servicemen. There for me was a coincidence for my own archaeological interests were stimulated by O. G. S. Crawford's writings... he a pioneer of research through air photography of ancient sites. He was one of Heligan's convalescers and is said to have written one of his books here.

World War II saw American officers in the house with their men encamped in the fields flanking the route to

Pentewan, all awaiting cross-channel orders after practising landings on the Winnick.

Sir John's solution for Heligan was to convert the mansion into flats, twenty two of them. The Cornwall Record Office manuscripts for this move are dated 1973-74. I selecting a flat in 1977, chose flat 12, and moved in during February 1978. I had then a wide choice as only about half the flats were occupied. What struck me at the time was that few residents seemed to be acquainted with the distinguished Service record of Sir John. But I did hear local Cornish gossip of royal interest in Heligan. King George V and Queen Mary came to the house in their post-Coronation Cornish visit, allegedly and possibly inaccurately because they were not enthralled with China Clay country. I was told that Commander Thomas, who did business with Heligan flowers sending them to Covent Garden, provided camellias for Princess Alexandra's wedding bouquet. The third piece of gossip was that Heligan was discussed as a possible residence for the Duke of Windsor and Mrs. Simpson.

The flat tenants related less to Sir John than to the administrator of Pentewan Sands, A. T. Rickeard who had the oversight, for the Tremayne family of Heligan, and for the initial resident caretaker, Frank Lloyd, and for the first gardener, part-time, Malcolm Stevens who lived in Palm Cottage adjacent to Heligan's stable-block.

In January 1983 the residents of Heligan formed themselves into a company, Heligan House Co. Ltd., and bought up the freehold of the house and its adjacent grounds, adding the Meadow to their purchase in order to safeguard the view to the south south east as far as the so-called 'Japanese Garden' with its visible large pond,— an important consideration as fourteen flats have windows, forty of them on that side, the 'Mevagissey Front' of the house.

The incorporation of the Meadow needed a definition of

its north east boundary between the 'Honey Pot', (the house's sewage works), and the pathway from Heligan's rear exit. On that boundary I was involved, as the creator of the Shrub Garden, though not consulted. In 1977 before coming to reside in the house, I offered to the Tremaynes' administrator a dozen of my Chingford, London, collection of Old Fashioned Roses, a gift for the garden close to the house. The negotiations were handled by my sister Madge, and I found my roses were given a site outside the area allocated for the residents' use. Also that gardener Stephens was not to plant or maintain my gift. So on my arrival I was committed to that task. And it spread for my initial rose area had been a vegetable allotment of John Hopwood, Flat 2, which the administrator and the other residents wished to eliminate. My gift area was under permanent attack by blackberry bushes spreading in from the untended area which was also bedevilled by elms with elm disease. So my efforts advanced till by 1983 "my" shrub garden was established, cleared of trouble and stocked with shrubs I bought or propagated from those I found in the neglected Tremayne woodland north west of the house....but also much enhanced by gifts from relatives and friends, especially Cornwall Garden Society folk, notably its then chairman Major Walter Magor of Lamellen and the head gardener of National Trust Trelissick, Barry Champion.

The Shrub Garden mistakenly termed my "hobby" by one resident was an unwelcome chore for me, though I gave it constant work. I was seventy when I started it, and though now in my eighties and banned from gardening by my doctor, I still perform, among the shrubs, jobs which do not involve bending. But my most personal interest was elsewhere, cultivating certain areas beside Grey Lady's Walk, at the top of the slope facing Heligan's front porch. I started the White Corner impelled by a gift of three shrubs from a resident, the late Harry

Wilden. Gifts from my son Kevin and friend Doris Smy, once my secretary and now an annual visitor to Heligan, helped to build up the White Corner. Moving to the north along the Walk, I planted other groups of shrubs, including camellias from Mrs. Margaret Miles, the then editor of Cornwall Garden, and at the far end of the walk, a group of camellias, four of them planted when my grandchildren were born... the group flanked by camellias from Major Magor and from Maisie's friend from her schoolgirl days, Kathleen Perry, retired head of a Training College.

The 1983 formation of Heligan House Co., saw an attempt to make me its first chairman, a job I managed to evade by being in hospital at the time. But I accepted the post of Vice-Chairman, having myself proposed the Rev. Geoffrey Powell, Flat 13, as Chairman. After six years he resigned and then I did take the chair stipulating one year only, 1989-1990.

The year 1990 saw the impact of Tim Smit of Gorran, a Dutch South African educated in Britain. It is said, I do not know if accurately, that he learned of the past glory of Heligan's woodland garden from my historical writings, initially notes borrowed from me by Major Magor and sent by him to editor Mrs. Margaret Miles for publication in the 'Cornwall Garden', No. 26 1983, "Heligan, Garden and Woodland", the first of a long series from me on Heligan history. Tim Smit persuaded J. R. T. Willis, Air Marshal Sir John Tremayne's grandson, to let him restore the woodland garden outside the area acquired by Heligan House Co., and to finance the project by opening the grounds involved to an entrance-paying public.

The initial reaction of most residents in Heligan House was not favourable to the venture as they feared invasion of privacy, but, as time passed, they accepted that the tourists encircled the house grounds at a distance, with minimal disturbance to the flat owners.

Let me finish with another coincidence. Soon after coming to live at Heligan, 1978, I was given a valuable list of notable Heligan trees compiled by Alan Mitchell of the Forestry Commission. Later I listened to Major Magor recalling how he accompanied Mitchell on various tree forays, including Heligan and Caerhays. The head of Kew was also involved in looking at Heligan trees with Major Magor.

So I was quite pleased to know that Tim Smit had succeeded in attracting Mitchell to Heligan's woodland garden to give the enterprise advice. There Mitchell heard of me from the other workers and wrote to me from his Surrey address reminding me that pre-World War II he was a pupil at Bancroft's School, Essex, and there I had been his history master.

I trust he was not affronted by my failure to recall him. In ten years as an assistant master in two Public Schools and twenty eight years as a Grammar School headmaster, I must have encountered between 2,000 and 3,000 pupils. And at the age of eighty five one of my weaknesses is a defective memory even of recent happenings.

Fortunately this account of Heligan depends not on memory but on my hundreds of notes made and filed over many years.

At this very moment 9:15. a.m. Sunday, December 26th 1993, when the B.B.C. is broadcasting the 'Letter from America' by Alastair Cooke, my friend and Cambridge contemporary, I am typing the last sentences of my more humble project which I can term "LETTERS FROM HELIGAN".